W9-ATZ-104

The Carnegie Endowment was founded in 1910 by Andrew Carnegie to promote international peace and understanding. To that end the Endowment conducts programs of research, discussion, publication and education in international affairs and American foreign policy. The Endowment also publishes the quarterly journal *Foreign Policy*.

As a tax-exempt operating foundation, the Endowment maintains a professional staff of Senior and Resident Associates who bring to their work substantial firsthand experience in foreign affairs. Through writing, public and media appearances, Congressional testimony, participation in conferences, and other activities, the staff engages the major policy issues of the day in ways that reach both expert and general audiences. Accordingly the Endowment seeks to provide a hospitable umbrella under which responsible analysis and debate may be conducted, and it encourages Associates to write and speak freely on the subjects of their work. The Endowment convenes special policy forums and, from time to time, issues reports of commissions or study groups.

The Endowment normally does not take institutional positions on public policy issues. It supports its activities principally from its own resources, supplemented by non-governmental, philanthropic grants.

FOREVER ENEMIES?

AMERICAN POLICY & THE ISLAMIC REPUBLIC OF IRAN

BY GEOFFREY KEMP

A CARNEGIE ENDOWMENT BOOK

Copyright © 1994 by
THE CARNEGIE ENDOWMENT FOR INTERNATIONAL PEACE
2400 N Street, NW, Washington, D.C. 20037
All Rights Reserved

Library of Congress Cataloging-in-Publication data
Kemp, Geoffrey
Forever Enemies?: American Policy and the
Islamic Republic of Iran/ by Geoffrey Kemp
p. cm.
"A Carnegie Endowment book."
Includes index.

ISBN 0-87003-036-1
1. United States—Foreign relations—Iran. 2.
Iran—Foreign relations—United States. I. Title.
E183.8.I55K42 1993
327.73055—dc20   93-43515 CIP

FOREWORD

It is fifteen years since the Islamic Revolution overthrew the Shah, well over four years since the death of the Ayatollah Khomeini and the end of the Iran-Iraq War, three years since Iraq's defeat in the Gulf War and the end of the Cold War, two years since the start of the Arab-Israeli peace talks, and six months since the Arafat-Rabin handshake. The dynamics of superpower relations, the Middle East, and Iran's domestic situation have changed, but have they changed enough to warrant a new direction in our Iranian policy?

Though Iran no longer commands much public attention, it remains key to security in the still vital and volatile Persian Gulf — a region that is home to half the world's known oil deposits, ethnic strife, Saddam's Iraq, a nascent Kurdish state, weak Arab governments and rampant uncertainty. And Iran itself continues to be a vexing problem for the United States.

It is, after all, not easy to deal with a government that refuses to talk to you but instead characterizes you in the most profane of terms, exports terrorism, and oppresses its own people. Adversity occasionally produces some flexibility; during Iran's dark days of 1985 and 1986 even Khomeini allowed his minions to engage in a form of dialogue with the U.S. government about trading arms for hostages. In the United States, however, a policy built on deception and lies, whatever its origin, could not be politically sustained.

One can be tempted, given the nature of the Iranian government and some of its conduct at home and abroad, to pursue a policy of confrontation short of hostilities. While professing our acceptance of the Islamic government, making that government's circumstances as difficult as possible in fact has been, in a not very concerted fashion, our policy for four successive administrations. Indeed, it has had a certain amount of success, though most specialists would argue it has done little to undermine the Mullahs. Combined with the Iranian government's own policy errors, our efforts have diminished the Iranian government's elan, its public support and its capabilities, but not its durability.

Today's post-revolutionary Iran is a war-weary state, grappling with political and social divisions at home, a fractured economy, and an unsettled neighborhood. But this has not ended a debate in Teheran about whether the government should be more concerned about spreading ideology than serving more mundane strategic, political and economic interests — interests which in some cases may not be antithetical to our own. Ironically perhaps, as Iran's internal circumstances grow more confused

and difficult, the world, including ourselves, has become increasingly dis-
inclined to add to the Iranian government's problems.

"Constructive engagement" tends to be an approach American officials
find generally appealing with any noxious government. It seeks to develop
mutual interests and a web of ties which will lead to overall better conduct. Sooner or later we may end up with such a policy if the Iranian government's popularity and effectiveness continue to decline and convincing interlocutors emerge. In all probability, the Islamic government's efforts to come to terms with a modern, interrelated world will bring
significant change to Iran, including its politics, in a number of years and
it will be prepared to do serious business with the West, including the
United States.

Problems to developing an Iranian policy

For the present, however, shaping an effective policy toward Iran is
difficult because of Iran's political uncertainties and its changeable domestic scene and because of our differences over Iran with our friends.
Moreover our ignorance — never small — of the country has grown as
our ability to interact with Iran has been all but eliminated. A long absence from Iran has severely diminished our intelligence capabilities and
our expertise. There is another major problem — it is difficult to have a
policy toward Iran when you do not have a policy toward Iraq. And that
has been lacking in Washington since the end of the Gulf War, unless
you consider waiting for something to turn up in Iraq to be a policy.

The advent of the Clinton administration offered a good opportunity
to take a fresh look at Iran. To that end, the Carnegie Endowment established a study group which met five times in 1992-93, chaired by Senior
Associate Geoffrey Kemp. The result is this broad policy review by Mr.
Kemp, which is his product alone, although it benefits from the deliberations of the study group.

Kemp provides a brief but comprehensive review of the basic elements
of our Iranian dilemma, its domestic uncertainties and diplomatic
difficulties, including the new considerations raised by the breakup of the
Soviet Union. He presents a realistic picture of Iran's problems, its capabilities and its serious limitations. He also offers insights into Iran's post-
Gulf War perceptions of its archenemy, the United States, now that
America "occupies both the regional and global driver's seat."

Kemp advocates resolute unilateral and multilateral pressures against
Iran's opposition to the Arab-Israel peace process, its support of terrorism and subversion, its human rights abuses, and, most importantly,
against its potential acquisition of nuclear and other unconventional
weapons. At the same time, he argues that we must accept the legitimacy

of the regime and be prepared to talk to its leaders at any time: "a dialogue should be regarded as the beginning of a long process to restore normalcy to relations between two countries too important to ignore each other." Iran should be offered the prospect of normal relations with the United States, including better economic ties, if points of contention can be resolved.

While Kemp is critical of the Clinton administration's "failure to reach a consensus with allies as the best way to stop Iran's unacceptable behavior," his proposals are generally consistent with the current lines of American policy, which itself follows the policy line of the previous administration.

Toughness combined with an offer of unconditional dialogue and selective constructive engagement, that is, potential progress in some very important areas for Iran, may well work if we are steadfast and patient. But our approach must entail a strategy for confronting the enormous nuclear risk posed by Iran: we and our allies must try to prevent or delay as long as possible the development of a nuclear capability. Iran has the personnel resources, the monies and the possible help from China and North Korea. We will not be happy even if a "moderate" Rafsanjani wields such a capacity. This is not a problem we can wish or trade or hide away as irrelevant to our domestic difficulties.

Lord Curzon once described religion in Persia as "inspiring at one moment the bigot's rage, at the next the agnostic's indifference." For the past fifteen years, Iran's Islamic government has given America much cause for outrage, and we ought to have learned that we cannot afford to respond with inattention or irresolve. Given our lack of knowledge of Iran, our declining attention to the strategically vital Gulf, and our apparent difficulties in mobilizing friends and allies, we could end up one bad day with a much bigger headache than the troublesome Iran we now face. Mr. Kemp's study contributes to the necessary effort to focus serious attention on our relations with Iran.

MORTON I. ABRAMOWITZ
President
Carnegie Endowment for International Peace

PREFACE

Between October 1992 and March 1993, the Carnegie Endowment organized a series of dinner meetings with a group of distinguished specialists to review American policy toward Iran. The ground rules of the meetings preclude listing the participants who included U.S. government officials and others working for international agencies. This book has benefitted greatly from the deliberations of the group. However it was decided at the outset that this would be a single author study. No attempt has been made to seek a consensus on this controversial topic. The views expressed are those of the author alone.

I owe great appreciation to Morton I. Abramowitz, President of the Endowment who not only urged me to organize the Study Group and write the book, but was an active participant in the deliberations and has made numerous editorial suggestions to improve the final manuscript. My closest collaborator in preparing this book has been Jeremy Pressman, Project Associate with Carnegie's Middle East Arms Control project. His contributions to the Study Group and the research and editing of the chapters, and the two detailed appendices which he wrote attest to his skills and dedication. I would also like to thank Caroline Drees, Paula Hacopian, Sanjay Kalpage and Michelle Sieff who, as full time Carnegie interns, made outstanding contributions to the project. Two volunteer interns, Eric Zandvliet and Steven Cook also provided very helpful inputs during the fall of 1993. I am grateful to Maria Alunan for her help in the early stages of the project, especially organizing the Study Group meetings.

Several colleagues in and out of government have provided me with insights into the subject matter or have read all, or part, of the manuscript and provided trenchant criticism at the right time. Of those I can mention, I offer special thanks to Shaul Bakhash, Jahangir Amuzegar, Shahram Chubin, Richard Haass, and Leonard Spector. Other thanks go to: David Merrill for his work on the maps, Rebecca Krafft for her skillful editing, Jane Firor for the cover design and layout, Jennifer Little and her extremely helpful and dedicated librarians, and Michael O'Hare, the Endowment's Director of Administration and Finance for his strong support and enthusiasm. Finally, my special thanks go to my indefatigable assistant Chris Bicknell, who has worked with me through the best of times and the most harried of times to finally bring this product to market.

GEOFFREY KEMP
Carnegie Endowment, February 1994

INTRODUCTION

On September 13, 1993, President Bill Clinton basked in glory on the
south lawn of the White House as the world watched him orchestrate an
unexpectedly pleasant event: the historic handshake between Israel's
Prime Minister Yitzhak Rabin and PLO Chairman Yasir Arafat. Eight
weeks later, in Iran, another event took place to remind Clinton that future Middle East encounters may be less congenial and will likely require
more of his time and energy.

On November 4, 1993, the 14th anniversary of the seizure of the U.S.
embassy, a major demonstration by followers of Supreme Religious
leader Ayatollah Ali Khamenei took place in Teheran denouncing the
United States and those Iranian officials who seek dialogue and better relations with Washington.[1] On November 24, Clinton met briefly in the
White House with British author Salman Rushdie who has been sentenced to death by Ayatollah Khomeini for writing *The Satanic Verses*.
George Bush had refused to meet with Rushdie during his tenure as president. The leadership in Teheran responded to the meeting by calling
Clinton "the most hated person before all Muslims of the world."[2]

Is this face-off the prelude to further confrontation between America
and Iran or can ways be found to reduce differences and avoid conflict?

Precisely because the issue of U.S.-Iranian relations is so contentious,
Clinton's instinct may well be to stay at arm's length from this problem
since coping with Iran exacted a heavy toll from his three immediate predecessors. The 1979-81 U.S. Embassy hostage crisis contributed greatly
to Jimmy Carter's electoral defeat in 1980; Ronald Reagan skirted im-
peachment in his second term in the fallout from the Iran-Contra affair;
and George Bush's role in that caper, though still unclear, may have ex-
pedited his own ouster in November 1992.

Nevertheless, strategic realities make Iran too important for the United States to ignore. Access to Persian Gulf oil will continue to be of vital
interest to the industrial world. While there are ways for the United
States to reduce this dependency significantly, no major reduction is likely to happen in this century. Instead the Western dependence on Persian
Gulf oil will continue to grow. Any hostile power that controls the Persian Gulf will be a threat to the West, hence the protection of the region
will remain a vital U.S. security concern for the rest of the decade, and
probably longer. This hypothetical threat was confirmed by Iraq's resource grab in 1990. Had Saddam Hussein been able to control the Arabian Peninsula's oil supplies, Iraq's economic problems would have been
solved at Western expense and its nuclear weapons program completed in
short shrift.

Likewise, the United States is too powerful and its Middle East presence too overwhelming for the Islamic Republic of Iran to ignore. Iran's leaders must decide whether head-to-head confrontation with the world's only superpower serves the interests of the revolution, or if some accommodation is both necessary and inevitable, especially if the Arab states and Israel finally bring an end to years of bloodshed and conflict by signing peace accords.

Both countries are aware that the Persian Gulf remains an unstable region. There are many troubling scenarios. Iraq could reemerge as a menace to the status quo if the U.N. embargo on Iraqi oil sales were lifted. Alternatively, a resurgent, more nationalist and authoritarian Russia could openly oppose U.S. policy and try to coerce Iran; upheavals on the Indian subcontinent could spill over into the Gulf; one or more of the conservative Arab regimes could be brought down and replaced by governments hostile to both Iran and the United States. Finally, a breakdown in the Arab-Israeli peace process could lead to a new Middle East war jeopardizing the entire region.

Regardless of who governs Iran, its history, geography and wealth assure its continued importance. Its prime geographic position, its great land area and large population ensure its ongoing role as a central player in Gulf affairs. Persia has existed for thousands of years and figured prominently in the development of world civilization. Even if a counter-revolution turned Iran into a pro-Western democracy, quarrels would likely persist with the West over such issues as oil production and pricing, as was the case when the Shah ruled Iran. For the present, the revolution seems entrenched and Iran's leaders continue to promote a radical ideology beyond their borders as a vehicle to sustain power internally.

Indeed, the Iranian regime has replaced Saddam Hussein's Iraq in the minds of many Americans as the most serious threat to U.S. and Western interests in the Middle East. With each passing day, highly negative stories appear in the Western media regarding Iran, accusing it of promoting terrorism in Europe and throughout the Middle East; undermining the Middle East peace process and denying Israel's right to exist; killing and torturing its own citizens; persecuting religious minorities especially the Baha'is; calling publicly for the murder of Salman Rushdie; and disputing territory and otherwise threatening pro-Western Arab governments in its neighborhood. In addition, the Western press has given repeated reminders that Iran is vilifying Western values, falling behind in its debt payments to foreign banks and, most ominously, undertaking a major arms buildup including sophisticated submarines, missiles, advanced combat aircraft and perhaps nuclear weapons.

Those who disagree with this characterization of Iranian behavior argue instead that it is Iran that is threatened and militarily insecure. Isolated internationally, Iran faces trouble on all its borders. To its west, north and east are dangerous or unstable regimes whose violent activities may spill over and undermine its own internal cohesion. To the south lies a suspicious group of rich Arab countries, well armed and protected by the world's remaining superpower. The Iranian regime has made efforts to improve its image with the world community, including the international financial institutions, but these have met with only muted success. Despite severe internal problems and widespread dissent among its leaders those who hold this view of a weaker Iran see American attempts to pressure the Iranian regime to change its ways as counterproductive.

At first glance the Clinton administration seems clearly to support the former view. Secretary of State Warren Christopher has asserted that the Clinton team has a "stronger policy of isolating Iran than the prior administration did. We think Iran is an international outlaw...and we're trying to persuade the other nations of the world to feel as we do, to treat Iran as an outlaw."[3] In reality however, there is less to this new American toughness than meets the eye. The administration has openly called for a dialogue with the Teheran regime and (though scarcely mentioned by administration officials) U.S. exports to Iran have increased dramatically over the past two years and include major sales of oil drilling and engineering equipment. Exports may reach $1 billion in 1993 compared to $747 million in 1992, $527 million in 1991 and $166 million in 1990. Iran is also selling huge amounts of oil to U.S. oil companies—between $3.5 billion and $4 billion a year—who sell it on the world market.[4] For this privilege the oil companies pay Iran in hard currency, which not only helps Iran's struggling economy but its rearmament program as well.

No matter how confusing the administration's policy may appear, there is no doubt that Iran poses a number of threats to American security interests. Most important are the possibility that the regime will eventually rebuild its military capabilities, possibly to include nuclear weapons, that it will continue efforts to subvert pro-Western Arab regimes and pursue its vehement rejection of Israel and the peace process.

This study calls for a centrist policy toward Iran. It advocates more assertive efforts to reach agreement with U.S. allies on curbing Iran's most provocative behavior. However it is also recommends that Iran be offered clear incentives to normalize relations with the West and become more engaged in constructive efforts to develop mutual security and arms control arrangements for the Persian Gulf.

In order to arrive at a basis for addressing the problem of U.S.-Iranian relations the elements of the policy debate must be set out in greater detail and the rhetoric distinguished from the substance. This is followed by a review of the key issues that condition U.S. and Iranian foreign policy and the difficulties these pose for efforts at reconciliation. The study concludes with a series of recommendations for American policy that take into account regional realities and the political constraints at work in both countries that preclude radical changes in their policies toward each other.

U.S. POLICY AND THE IRANIAN CHALLENGE

U.S. policy toward Iran is couched in broader American interests and goals in the Middle East: a resolution to the Arab-Israeli conflict, a change of regime in Iraq and the security of the Persian Gulf and its oil supplies. If Israel and its Arab neighbors, especially Syria, make peace as a result of the Israeli-PLO agreement reached in September 1993, they will have achieved a huge step toward a more stable Middle East. Should this come to pass, Iran's ability to stir up trouble by exploiting ties with extremist groups in Lebanon, Israel and the occupied territories would be diminished. An Arab-Israeli peace would make it easier for most Arab regimes to cooperate with the United States on other Middle East issues. Similarly, if Saddam Hussein's regime were eventually replaced by more amenable rulers, Iraq could reemerge as a counterweight to Iran by virtue of its geography and wealth.

These, however, are optimistic scenarios. A full-fledged Arab-Israeli peace and a more palatable regime in Baghdad will not come into being overnight. In the meantime, a more focused Iran policy would, if successful, limit the revolutionary regime's potential for undermining these broader goals and also establish the basis for better U.S.-Iranian relations.

Given Iran's capacity for troublemaking, which will be much greater if it strengthens its military base, is it wise for the United States to accelerate initiatives to isolate the Islamic Republic, along with Iraq, and cast them as two equally hostile regional outcasts? Or, is there now an opportunity to articulate a less contentious approach with Teheran while continuing to pursue a hard line against Saddam Hussein? The Clinton administration's willingness to confront Iranian behavior reflects the belief, shared by most Iran watchers, that Iran is currently weak and unable to challenge the United States in any direct manner. However, precisely for this reason critics of the administration believe a less confrontational policy would be more likely to change Iranian behavior.

The Islamic Republic sends contradictory signals as to its real intentions. Infighting among its leadership has generated haphazard and inconsistent foreign policies as rival forces assert their dominance and influence in particular areas. As a result, the most contentious arguments about the adequacy of U.S. policy center on competing interpretations of the divisiveness within the Iranian body politic. In short, does there exist a genuine choice between radicals and moderates, or are the moderates merely a more pragmatic breed of revolutionaries, with a hidden, but expansionist, anti-Western agenda?

CURRENT U.S. POLICY TOWARD IRAN

An overview of U.S. relations with Iran reveals two seemingly contradictory trends. The legal and diplomatic framework appears tough and restrictive, but economic statistics suggest a more cooperative U.S.-Iranian relationship. This dichotomy, inherited from previous administrations, may help explain why Clinton officials have had trouble charting a single course for U.S.-Iranian relations.

A wide array of executive and legislative constraints imposed between 1979 and 1993 by the Carter, Reagan and Bush administrations blocks most military and many economic transactions between the two countries. Major categories of dual-use technology exports have been banned since Iran was placed on the State Department's list of state supporters of terrorism in 1984. With the exception of just a few items, imports from Iran have been illegal since 1987. No bilateral diplomatic relations exist, and the United States has maintained a continuous state of national emergency with respect to Iran since the hostage taking of 1979. The Iran-Iraq Arms Non-Proliferation Act of 1992 reinforced and expanded the restrictions.

Yet U.S. exports to Iran have steadily increased over the last few years from zero in 1989 to a projected $1 billion in 1993. And by purchasing Iranian oil and refining it outside the United States, U.S. oil companies have legally injected $3.5 billion into the Iranian economy. Hence the reconstruction of Iranian oil production facilities is proceeding with the help of U.S. firms. Moreover, documents declassified by the House Foreign Affairs Committee have revealed that from August 1991 through February 1992, the U.S. Department of Commerce licensed sales of digital computers, radar testing equipment, computer software and inertial-navigation equipment.[1] Though some of these specific items are now apparently banned, this large-scale and legal trade between Iran and the United States contrasts vividly with the restrictive laws and orders on record; it also suggests a much more relaxed attitude to commercial ties than was ever permitted during the Cold War containment of the Warsaw Pact countries.[2]

U.S. actions—official policy and commercial realities—send different messages to Americans and Iranians. (This is an ironic twist given frequent U.S. complaints that the Iranian government speaks in many voices). Consider, for instance, the debate over a proposed sale of commercial jets by Boeing to Iran. Those in favor of saving American jobs, realize that European competitors will sell the Airbus if given any chance; to them a presidential decision in favor of the Boeing sale makes sense.

Others who reject the idea of contributing to Iran's technological growth as long as it remains a threat, see blocking the sale as essential.

The administration's formal pronouncements have not dispelled the confusion. On May 18, 1993, Martin Indyk, the senior director for the Near East and South Asia on the National Security Council, explained that the Clinton policy of "dual containment" was derived from "an assessment that the current Iraqi and Iranian regimes are both hostile to American interests in the region."[3] Indyk distinguished Clinton's policy from previous ones: consigning American interests in the Middle East to a local balance of power between the key regional countries, a policy pursued by successive administrations prior to the Gulf War, was inadequate; America's interests there were too important. Dual containment would also entail an enhanced American military commitment to the Gulf with closer military ties to such key powers as Saudi Arabia and Turkey. Indyk was careful to avoid appearing overly harsh adding that the Clinton administration does not oppose Islamic government in Iran, only "specific aspects" of the regime's behavior and that current U.S. policy does not seek a confrontation with Iran.

Indyk's only concrete proposal was to persuade Europe and Japan to help prevent Iran from acquiring weapons. Unfortunately the phrase "dual containment" took on a life of its own by virtue of its direct allusion to the Cold War and the containment of communism. And by lumping Iran and Iraq together in the same nefarious camp, it also implied that the United States had similar policies toward both countries when in fact they are very different on key issues (Figure I). By late May, the media was trumpeting the impending isolation of Iran by the United States.[4] Secretary of State Christopher continued discussing a policy of dual containment. On June 9, 1993, he met with European allies in Luxembourg to plead for "a collective policy of containment to halt Iran's nuclear and chemical weapons program."[5] The European countries agreed to study the situation.

By late July, perhaps because of the media's narrow focus on the term "dual containment," the administration's tone had softened. In testimony before the Europe and Middle East Subcommittee of the House Foreign Affairs Committee, Edward Djerejian, assistant secretary of state for Near East affairs, stated that "we do not seek a total embargo or quarantine of Iran ....We do not seek to overturn the Iranian government....Our policy does not exclude dialogue with Iran....Our offer of a dialogue with authorized Iranian representatives remains valid. We have no preconditions for such a dialogue." When asked if this was a policy of containment, he

Figure 1   U.S. Policy Toward Iraq and Iran

	Iraq	Iran
Similarities	No diplomatic relations with U.S. Military and terrorist threat to U.S. and allies	
Differences	U.N. embargo on most items	Limited U.S. unilateral embargo on selected items
	No commerce with United States	Growing trade relations with the United States
	U.S. *rejects* dialogue with Saddam Hussein	U.S. *wants* dialogue with Teheran regime
	U.S. wishes to remove Saddam Hussein's regime	U.S. accepts legitimacy of regime
	U.S. military operations periodically conducted against the regime	No recent U.S. military activity against Iranian forces

replied: "It's a policy focusing on how to alter Iranian behavior...." He refrained from using the words "containment" or "isolation."[6]

In March 1994, the concept of dual containment reemerged when National Security Advisor Anthony Lake wrote in *Foreign Affairs* that Iran and Iraq are two of a handful of "backlash" states. The United States has a responsibility to "neutralize, contain and, through selective pressure, eventually transform" these countries. In the Iranian case, the United States seeks an "authoritative" dialogue in which the United States "will raise aspects of Iranian behavior that cause us so much concern." Lake categorically rejects positive inducements "such as trade and aid concessions or rescheduling of loans." In an attempt to avoid earlier criticism, Lake explains that dual containment does not mean "duplicate containment."[7]

Considering the difficulties and failures that have beset the last three presidents, it is not surprising that President Clinton has had a hard time formulating a consistent and effective policy toward Iran. The rhetoric has been both harsh and conciliatory. How to balance tough laws with economic realities remains a quandary. In essence then, the basic policy of past administrations has gone largely unchanged by this one. This having been said, there are concrete policy alternatives for the United States, and these deserve further exploration.

TWO ALTERNATIVE POLICIES

The most vocal critics of American policy fall into two general groups: those who believe current policy is wrong because it exaggerates the Iranian threat and prescribes counterproductive measures, and those who think it is not tough enough. What follows are summaries of the main arguments these critics make: the Olive Branch and Expanded Confrontation.

The Olive Branch[8]

Critics who regard U.S. policies as strident and not in the best interests of America and the international community include a number of senior Iranian specialists in the United States and otherwise pro-American foreigners including many officials from Europe, Japan and Russia. They argue that Iran is less of a threat than is often supposed, that its behavior can change and therefore that the United States should rethink its current policy of confrontation with the Islamic Republic. Instead, the United States should seek a new relationship with Teheran by establishing a dialogue and revising current U.S. executive policy and laws. Regional developments have rendered such an approach all the more urgent in view of the increasing polarization in the Middle East between moderates and extremists, the failure of pro-Western Arab regimes to solve their domestic problems and the growing number of conflicts in the Caucasus and Central Asia that find Iran and Russia sharing similar goals.

According to this school, the administration is misinterpreting Iranian actions and misunderstanding or perhaps underestimating, the regime's inherent weaknesses, especially in the economic sphere. In support of this view, critics characterize the Islamic Republic as having lost its revolutionary fervor. Now a debtor nation, its per capita GDP is but 57 percent of what it had been under the Shah. Its priority must therefore be economic reconstruction in the wake of the disastrous war with Iraq and the domestic upheaval of the Khomeini period. President Rafsanjani represents a more pragmatic and open approach to problem solving. He is willing to work more closely with the West than his predecessors but he faces much domestic opposition, in part because of the poor performance of the economy. Nevertheless, Iran is sufficiently strong (it pumps roughly 3.5 million barrels of oil a day) that hopes of changing or overthrowing the regime are unrealistic. Furthermore, if Iran is isolated and unfairly stigmatized as the source of all evil in the Middle East, the worst American expectations could become self-fulfilling prophesies. Iran and so-called Islamic fundamentalism make easy targets for Western animosity, but such stereotyping is simplistic and gratuitous. The first task of the United States should be to understand Iran and the meaning of Islamic revivalism.

Essential to the Olive Branchers' view is the perception that inherent Iranian hostility and aggressiveness is, in part, externally created. Iranian behavior may be understood as the actions of a large but beleaguered state. Iran is pursuing its national interest in much the same way as it has in the past. If the United States finds this threatening, then it will never be able to deal with Iran or any other important country that is just recovering from a long and costly war in which it was the loser.

According to this reasoning, Iran's military buildup is justified given its arms and equipment losses during the Iran-Iraq War and any informed opinion of Iran should take into account the wars and chaos to its west, north and east as well as the hostile Arab countries to its south, which are engaged in an arms spending spree that includes purchases of advanced U.S. weapons. Most threatening, America maintains a large military presence in the region. In this view, Iran's purchases of advanced conventional equipment from Russia are conditioned by certain facts: they are based on agreements signed more than four years ago and the weapons are being offered at a reasonable price. Iran is reacting as any state would in such a situation. Olive Branchers dispute that there is any hard evidence to date of an Iranian nuclear weapons program or other weapons of mass destruction. They find it noteworthy that Iran, unlike most of the Arab countries, has signed the Chemical Weapons Convention.

Although it is true that Iranian opposition to the Arab-Israeli peace process and its rejection of Israel pose problems, Olive Branch proponents see these postures as tactical maneuvers necessary to keep Iranian radicals in line. If Israel and the Arabs (including the Palestinians) were to reach a political settlement, Iran could do nothing to influence it and ultimately would have to accept Israel's right to exist. Iranian leaders would be more likely to move in this direction if they had a better rapport with the United States rather than overt confrontation with it. Although Iran's record on human rights is poor, it is probably better than Saudi Arabia's and those of several other U.S. regional clients who deny their citizens the most elementary rights and permit none of the open political debate found every day in the Iranian parliament.

According to the Olive Branchers, it is in American interests to work with the Islamic Republic to modify its more extreme policies. This can only happen if the United States reassesses its own policies which have clearly failed. A great opportunity to do so was missed at the end of the 1991 Gulf War. Iran's behavior during the war had been cautious and responsible, and Iranian intervention was instrumental in the long-awaited release of the Western hostages from Lebanon. Had the United States made a gesture to Iran at that time to discuss regional security and arms control, many of the misunderstandings about the current military buildup in the region might have been averted. Such rejection of Iran's goodwill gestures strengthens the hand of Iranian radicals and discourages moderation and cooperation.

In the Olive Branch approach, specific U.S. policies can be changed to build a new relationship with Iran without compromising U.S. interests or principles. A first step would be the removal of a morass of technical obstacles, including the final settlement of the arbitration claims made by the two countries over asset appropriations dating back to the 1979 crisis. Another step would be to end State Department objections to the sale of U.S. commercial aircraft to Iran. The technologies of jet airliners, such as the Boeing 737 or Airbus 300, have nothing to do with either missile production or nuclear weapons. The European Airbus consortium would welcome an Iranian offer to buy their aircraft and clearly Russia would eagerly act on the chance to penetrate this market. Thus, denying such sales to U.S. companies merely penalizes American workers and does nothing to limit Iran's expansion of its commercial air fleet. The logic of blocking the sale is directly contradicted by the millions of dollars of U.S. sales of oil production equipment to Iran, which U.S. laws permit, and which does far more to strengthen Iran's military program than commercial aircraft sales.

The observers believe that now is the time to pursue a bold new policy, especially while Iran's military capabilities are still weak. Enacting hard line policies will only strengthen the radicals and make a future confrontation all the more dangerous and inevitable throughout the Middle East. The United States should accept that Islamic revivalism is under way in most Muslim countries from Algeria to Saudi Arabia as a backlash against poverty and incompetent, corrupt regimes. It is not orchestrated by Teheran, even though Iran welcomes the phenomenon.

A final, key point in the Olive Branch view is that Iran is too important a country for the United States to be engaged in a continuous confrontation. Increasing disagreements with key U.S. allies, particularly the Russians, the Europeans and the Japanese, forebode the isolation of the United States if it continues its current policy. In contrast, the Olive Branch represents a clean break with failed policies of past U.S. administrations. It would likely attract considerable support in the region, particularly from those Arab countries concerned about the possibility of a grassroots backlash against the American presence. It reflects a more mature and sensitive U.S. attitude to Islamic challenges. It puts the onus on Iran to respond positively to American openings and to get its own house in order. If such a policy does not work, the United States could then better make the case for Iran's isolation.

Expanded Confrontation[9]
Another group of analysts and advocates believes the Clinton administration is not tough enough and should go farther in escalating the confrontation with Iran. These Expanded Confrontationists feel no concessions can be made to the Iranian regime. They see the Islamic Republic as determined to undermine Western interests in the Middle East, to pursue a nuclear weapons option and to continue to use terrorism against its opponents at home and abroad. Iran's propensity for regional hegemony is evident in its behavior toward the Arab states of the Gulf and its arms buildup. Since Iran is a revolutionary state, these observers believe there can be no accommodation with the regime. Nothing short of its demise would serve Western interests. The stakes are so high that they justify as

strong a means as possible to challenge Iran, thereby averting an otherwise inevitable Middle East crisis and possibly a new war.

Expanded Confrontationists hold that the Iranian regime is on a collision course with the West, both from an ideological and geopolitical perspective. The United States should highlight these ideological distinctions. Radical Islam (in its many guises) is a threat to Western interests, be it in Algeria, Egypt, the Sudan or Iran itself. Given the fragility of the states of the Arab Gulf, social upheavals in key countries, including Saudi Arabia, cannot be ruled out. The possibility of Iranian hegemony in the absence of strong countervailing Western pressure would be high.

Five years from now, or even sooner, these observers fear that Iran could pose the sort of threat to the Arabian Peninsula that Iraq did in the summer of 1990. The Clinton administration, they warn, cannot afford to make the same mistake as the Bush administration—underestimating Iran the way U.S. officials misjudged Iraq. Although the Iranian military buildup has not yet reached the level of Iraq's in 1990, the Iranian political capacity for interference and undermining legitimate Arab governments is more sophisticated than that of Saddam Hussein and his entourage. Therefore, confrontation with Iran requires not only dealing with the direct military problems, which, for the time being, are manageable, but with the political threats. Only a strong American presence in the Gulf would assure this capability. Furthermore, Iran's potential military challenge to the United States is likely to become more formidable, especially its threat to U.S. maritime power. Fighting a future major war against a fully rearmed Iran would be more difficult than taking on Iraq was.

In the Expanded Confrontationists' view, the menace the Islamic Republic represents for Israel is unrelenting. The Iranian regime, in keeping with its radical Islamic ideology, regards Israel as an illegitimate entity that is unacceptable under any circumstances, hence the Arab-Israeli peace process is an aberration to be stopped. In the same way, Iran uses Islam to justify the death sentence on Salman Rushdie. To counter these challenges, Expanded Confrontation calls on the United States to mount a political campaign against Iran; Islam, in its more extreme form, has replaced communism as a major threat to the West. It is in fact more insidious since some of the attributes of radical Islam are appealing to fundamentalists of all religious persuasions. Consequently, it is in the Western interest not merely to modify and restrict the behavior of the Islamic Republic but to work to undermine the regime and, if necessary, plan for its overthrow. And now is the time to mount such a campaign: the regime is weak, the mullahs are in trouble, and further pressure on the Iranian economy could bring about an internal uprising.

While some U.S. allies may initially balk at this approach, strong American leadership could persuade them, if not to change their minds, at least to remain neutral. The United States could coordinate a strategy embracing Israel, the moderate Arab states and Iranian opposition groups in order to defeat the Rafsanjani regime and to further isolate it in the international community. The Central Intelligence Agency could develop a comprehensive covert action program against Iran. U.S. representatives at the United Nations could work closely with Security Council allies to find ways to delegitimize the Rafsanjani regime and give more support to Iranian opposition groups. The International Atomic Energy Agency and other international organizations could be convinced to take measures to stop the nuclear program with the same vigor that the United States pursued Operation Staunch in the 1980s preventing Iran's access to military-related technology. The United States should use its clout in the international organizations to deny Iran concessional loans from the international financial institutions. U.S. laws that permit retaliation against foreign companies and governments that sell prohibited items to Iran (and Iraq) should be enforced with maximum publicity.

Those supporting this argument believe that it is coherent and straightforward and if pursued with determination, could neutralize dissent from key allies. These advocates insist that regimes such as the Islamic Republic are an anathema to Western interests and to the new world order and there can be no accommodation with them. A hard line policy sets clear guidelines for executive and legislative action, and it might also give a strong boost to opposition groups and stimulate further dissidence within Iran.

SHORTCOMINGS OF THE THREE APPROACHES

While these three approaches—current U.S. policy and the two alternatives—contain some sensible and overlapping observations and proposals, each has its drawbacks. Underlying the benign Olive Branch approach is the assumption that an ideological regime like the Islamic Republic wants to live in concert with the West and its many pro-Western neighbors. Yet there is little evidence to support this proposition. The regime has failed to rein in its most extreme factions. In fact, following his weak showing in the June 1993 elections, Rafsanjani had to offer key cabinet posts to dedicated hard liners. Thus, the regime seems bound by its own ideology to challenge the legitimacy of Western concepts, including the secularism found in Turkey and the multiconfessionalism that has been the cornerstone of Lebanon's constitution. Indeed, in the case of Lebanon, the Iranian regime continues to arm and train Hizbollah, an organization whose avowed agenda is the establishment of an Islamic Republic in Lebanon and open confrontation with Israel, a state it regards as illegitimate. The Israeli-Palestinian agreement of September 1993 was met with disdain and derisive rhetoric and there are reports of increasing Iranian involvement with Sudan, an Islamic regime which the United States has added to its list of states that support international terrorism.

Second, while there is some evidence that radical nationalist Middle East regimes have, over time, become more accepting of a Western presence and given lip service to key Western values including democracy and human rights, the track record for radical Islamic regimes is less promising. There is no more reason to believe that the Iranian regime will willingly abandon its confrontational theology than to have faith that Libya's Colonel Muammer Gaddafy is a reformable person, or that the extremist Islamic factions fighting to control Afghanistan will become model democrats. Furthermore, even if the Iranian regime were to change its spots, other observers raise the issue that a more "pragmatic" Iran would pose just as many problems for the West and could, under certain circumstances, prove to be a more formidable foe. The reason? A more nationalist Iran would pursue a geopolitical rather than ideological agenda with an emphasis on economic growth. This could strengthen its propensity to extend its hegemony in the Gulf and areas of Central Asia.[10]

Third, there is no evidence that demarches and concessions to Iran, without prior changes in Iranian policy, will achieve positive results. Rather, they may embolden the regime to step up its overall anti-Western agenda. Iran is only likely to change its policy concerning the issues that arouse such antagonism with the United States—namely nuclear weapons, terrorism, fundamentalist ideology and the Middle East peace process—if greater pressure is applied.

While those who advocate the Olive Branch make some powerful arguments and some of their recommendations are sensible, it is unrealistic to expect the administration to adopt such a radical departure from recent U.S. policy. President Clinton can no more contemplate major concessions to Iran than he can propose normalization of relations with Saddam Hussein. Iran has a long way to go to redeem itself in American eyes before any significant gestures can be made. Furthermore, the Olive Branch would be unacceptable to Israel and several of the key Arab countries, especially Egypt and Saudi Arabia, all of which are increasingly concerned about Iranian political activity and its long-range military program.

Equally unacceptable is the Expanded Confrontation approach. Support for such tough measures might be more forthcoming if Iranian behavior were to change for the worse in unambiguous ways. But absent such a deterioration, its draconian prescriptions are impractical. They far exceed the measures advocated by the Clinton administration and would be bitterly criticized by foreign commerce ministries in Europe, Japan and Russia, who do not share the U.S. perspective and would shrink from the U.S. lead in such a confrontation. Such disagreement and division would limit the effectiveness of U.S. actions, including military operations, and strengthen the resolve of radicals throughout the Middle East to resist the United States. This could result in a major increase in terrorism, threatening not only American lives but the very foundations of U.S. Middle East policy including the Arab-Israeli peace process.

As for the Clinton policy, if the administration's efforts to limit Iran's military program and the support for terrorism and subversion are to be successful, the cooperation of key allies such as Europe, Russia and Japan is essential. Together they must be able to galvanize enough political clout to neutralize the errant behavior of such countries as the People's Republic of China and North Korea who are selling Iran dangerous technology. But this is exceedingly difficult to manage as long as Iran has access to hard currency and is trading with the rest of the world, including the United States. If the Clinton administration were truly serious about isolating Iran, it should end all commercial exports and forbid U.S. oil companies from buying Iranian oil. But the opposite is happening; U.S. exports of key products that help Iran re-establish its oil industry are increasing and nothing is being done to stop the purchase of Iranian oil. The most the United States can hope to do is to prevent Iran from getting certain key technologies that relate to weapons of mass destruction, and this task will not be easy.

Another risk with the Clinton policy is that it places increasing reliance on U.S. military power as the chosen instrument to deter both Iran and Iraq from aggressive behavior at a time when the pressures to cut the U.S. defense budget are strong and Clinton's abilities as commander-in-chief are being questioned. To make deterrence credible, the United States must expand its military relations with the key regional allies. This requires more access agreements to preposition equipment and supplies, including ammunition; more joint training exercises and joint planning with local forces; and more and better coordinated arms sales to the Gulf Cooperation Council (GCC) and other allies. However, if military relations between the United States and the GCC become too close, and there is no political resolution to the Gulf conflicts, there is the possibility of negative political fallout throughout the Islamic world which could be exploited by Iran and Iraq.

America's dominant military presence in the region and the absence, for the time being, of a serious competitor, should not give rise to complacency. Russia, Iraq and Iran all have the potential and the will to challenge America in the future. As Zbigniew Brzezinski has written, "current American supremacy in the Middle East is built, quite literally, on sand."[11]

Finally, the Clinton approach offers Iran few incentives to change its behavior aside from the promise of "dialogue." If the regime were in serious jeopardy, as Castro's Cuba is, such an approach could be justified on the grounds that nothing should be done perpetuate it. However most indicators suggest that no matter how unpopular the mullahs are, there is little likelihood that the regime will fall in the foreseeable future. The Clinton policy offers Iran no road map to show how, and in what areas, relations could improve in the event of a constructive dialogue.

A CENTRIST POLICY TOWARD IRAN

If each of these alternatives is flawed, what policy does make sense for the United States? The United States must adopt a long-term, realistic strategy in consultation with our key allies and with their cooperation. The realities of the region suggest this can only work if a highly pragmatic and future-oriented approach to policy is taken. The remainder of this study focuses on the reasons why a centrist policy toward Iran that contains both rewards and penalties is not only necessary, it is more likely to work than other approaches.

To make this case, five relevant areas are examined. First, the checkered history of recent U.S.-Iranian relations is reviewed; a picture emerges of strong, mutually reinforcing psychological barriers that prevent any easy transition to normalized relations. Second, the current divisions within Iran's ruling elite are examined to show how disputes over domestic policy influence Iran's foreign relations and why, at this time, it is difficult for the pragmatists led by President Rafsanjani to respond to American calls for an official dialogue. Third, Iran's complicated and ambiguous relations with its neighbors are evaluated, indicating that despite the fears Gulf Arab countries express about Iranian hegemony, most seek better relations with Teheran and still regard Baghdad as the greater security threat. To the north, Iran's relations with Turkey and Russia tend to be relatively cordial and it is argued that all three countries wish to work together to avoid confrontation over conflicts in the Caucasus and Central Asia. Fourth, the nature and consequences of Iran's military programs and its support for radical anti-Western groups are examined; if Iran's nuclear program expands it will pose very serious problems for the United States. On the other hand, Iran's conventional rearmament program has yet to develop into a serious threat. If certain weapons acquisitions continue, however, this could change—with dangerous consequences. Iran's continued support for terrorism and subversion guarantees continued American enmity. Iran's human rights abuses are covered and reveal that, no matter what excuses are made for the regime, its record on this matter is very poor. The study concludes with specific recommendations for U.S. policy, including suggested measures to counter the most serious threats—nuclear weapons, subversion and opposition to the Middle East peace process—as well as suggested initiatives to encourage Iran's pragmatists to enter into a meaningful dialogue with American officials.

THE ROOTS OF AMERICAN- IRANIAN ENMITY

Iran and the United States have dozens of reasons to distrust each other. One reason concerns the close relationship the two countries sustained for over forty years and the abrupt manner in which it came to an end with the revolution in 1979. Other reasons stem from the volatile and flagrantly hostile relations that have prevailed since that time.

WORLD WAR II: FROM NEUTRAL TO STRATEGIC ALLY

Although Iran, or Persia as it was then known, declared neutrality at the outbreak of World War II, the Iranian government was sympathetic to Germany. The British and Soviet governments demanded that the Iranian government expel several thousand German advisors present in the country. Iran's leader, Reza Shah Pahlavi, procrastinated; on August 25, 1941, 60,000 Soviet and British troops invaded Iran and defeated the Iranian army in a series of quick battles.

The Allies forced the Shah to abdicate in September 1941, and his son, Mohammed Reza Pahlavi, ascended to the throne. For the remainder of the war, Iran was controlled by Soviet troops in the north, British troops in the south and a joint force on the outskirts of Teheran. In late 1941, U.S. forces arrived in Iran to provide support for the "Persian corridor," a key access route for providing lend-lease to the Soviet Union. A year later, U.S. forces moved from an auxiliary role under the British forces to assuming direct responsibility for transferring the supplies. Between November 1941 and September 1945, a total of 4,159,117 long tons of cargo from the Western hemisphere was shipped to the Soviet Union through the Persian Gulf. This represents nearly one-quarter (23.8 percent) of the goods and supplies that the Soviet Union received during its involvement in World War II.[1]

POSTWAR U.S. RELATIONS WITH IRAN

Soviet maneuvers in northern Iran precipitated the first crisis of the Cold War. Unlike the United States and Great Britain, the Soviet Union was unwilling to withdraw its forces from Iran. Instead, Soviet troops backed the rebellious Tudeh Party and the Tudeh-led government in the Azerbaijan province. The Soviet Union's demands included autonomy for the province and generous oil concessions from the Iranian government. In December 1945, Azerbaijani leaders established an autonomous state with the help of Soviet troops. The troops were eventually pulled out as a result of Western pressure, U.N. action and favorable Soviet-Iranian agreements. A year after it was founded, the autonomous Azerbaijani state collapsed as Iranian forces took control of the province.

In 1951, the Iranian government nationalized the Anglo-Iranian Oil Company which had been jointly owned by Britain and Iran. Tension over control of the company had been building for several years because Britain was getting more revenue from taxes on company profits than Iran received in royalties. When Prime Ministers Ali Razmara and Hussein Ala failed to satisfy the Iranian public's demand for nationalization of the oil company, they were forced aside. Violent demonstrations were held in support of the Majles' (parliament's) demand that the Shah appoint Mohammed Mossadegh, a leading proponent of nationalization, as premier. Relations between Iran and the West became increasingly embittered. Mossadegh became prime minister on April 29, 1951, and implemented the Anglo-Iranian takeover and other policies unpopular in the West. An oil embargo against Iran by most European shippers was put into effect and had a crippling impact on the Iranian economy. In August 1953, the United States and Britain helped to overthrow Mossadegh and restore the Shah to full power.

The Shah was determined to ally with the West. Iran joined the Baghdad Pact in October 1955 along with Iraq, Turkey, Pakistan and Great Britain. The United States, though not officially a member of the pact, joined several of the committees. In 1958 Secretary of State John Foster Dulles told the members of the Baghdad Pact that the Eisenhower Doctrine, which had been announced in March 1957 and promised U.S. action to counter communist subversion in the Middle East, committed the United States to their defense as effectively as would actual U.S. membership in the pact. Following a coup in Baghdad on July 14, 1958, which overthrew the pro-Western monarchy, Iraq withdrew from the pact in 1959, and the remaining members renamed it the Central Treaty Organization (CENTO). In March 1959, the United States and Iran concluded a bilateral pact pledging cooperation in promoting the security and defense of CENTO members.

The Kennedy administration believed that American interests would be better served if the Iranian government had more domestic legitimacy and less corruption. Kennedy informed the Shah in 1962 that future U.S. aid would emphasize long-term economic development rather than military strength. The Shah was disturbed by the American demands. He was especially worried about the American reluctance to underwrite the cost of upgrading Iranian military forces to a level necessary to match those of his now hostile neighbor, Iraq. However, the Shah was willing to make concessions: he accepted the cutback in military aid and launched his White

Revolution of economic and social reform in January 1963. At the same time, he decided to pursue a more independent course in foreign affairs.

The White Revolution met with opposition from religious leaders and landlords, eventually leading to rioting in Teheran in June 1963. The Shah took advantage of these events to neutralize overt opposition, and he emerged with considerable strength internally, giving him more confidence in pursuing his own foreign policy.

In 1964 President Johnson agreed to provide Iran with foreign military sales credits because it was determined these would not cause excessive diversion of resources from development needs. Between 1964 and 1969, Iran's economy continued to grow (primarily from oil exports) and the program was terminated in 1969 after Iran acquired the means to finance procurement of its defense needs.

Meanwhile, Britain's historic decision in 1968 to terminate its military role east of the Suez brought about a reassessment of the American role in the Gulf and a qualitative and quantitative change in the U.S.-Iranian military relationship. Iran and key Arab states, especially Saudi Arabia, resolved to increase their military forces to deter outside intervention and prevent anti-monarchist forces from exploiting the power vacuum left by Britain's departure. At this time, the United States reviewed its Persian Gulf policy and decided that despite its strong interest in the stability and independence of the region it would not try to fill the void left by Britain with an increased U.S. military presence. Instead, the Nixon administration opted to rely on local powers. As a result, the United States adopted the twin-pillar policy built on cooperation with Iran and Saudi Arabia. Of the two pillars, Iran was by far the more important from a military perspective.

During the 1970s, regional players benefitted from the explosion in oil prices and the subsequent bonanza in hard currency revenues available for military purchases. This, in turn, allowed a dramatic acceleration of Iran's defense buildup as it purchased billions of dollars worth of sophisticated front-line American military equipment.[3]

THE REVOLUTION AND ITS FALLOUT

In January 1979, the Shah was overthrown. The Iranian revolution and the advent of the Khomeini regime elicited a swift American response that has toughened unremittingly over the years. At the time of the revolution, hundreds of millions of dollars' worth of military equipment ordered and paid for by the Shah was embargoed, and the financing, which had been prepaid, was impounded. The Iranian military establishment, particularly the air force, had to struggle to acquire spare parts as the

United States gradually tightened the noose on follow-up sales and servicing, especially after Iranian radicals captured the U.S. Embassy in
Tehran on November 4, 1979, and, with government approval, held
American diplomats hostage for more than fourteen months. President
Carter issued an executive order declaring a national emergency with respect to U.S.-Iranian relations and less than half a year later, as the crisis
dragged on, he broke diplomatic relations with Iran.

The hostage crisis, which lasted until January 1981, represented a
nadir in U.S.-Iranian relations, bottoming out with the failed American
military rescue mission, Desert One, on April 24, 1980. Desert One,
along with the unexpected Soviet invasion of Afghanistan the previous
Christmas, provoked a change in the Carter administration's attitudes
and policies toward the Gulf region. One result was the Carter Doctrine;
it stated that the United States was prepared to use force if either the Soviet Union or Iran threatened Gulf oil. Carter's newfound support for a
tougher line on the defense of the Middle East left an enduring mark on
American policy toward Iran. The Rapid Deployment Joint Task Force
was established in 1979 and the basic contingency plan for fighting a war
against the Soviet Union was codified with the front line of defense
drawn in Iran's Zagros Mountains.[4]

In January 1981, literally as the Reagan administration was taking
office, the hostage crisis was resolved. As part of the settlement, the United States-Iran Claims Tribunal at The Hague was set up to adjudicate
outstanding financial claims. Banks, governments, companies and individuals all sought to recover damages, contract payments and lost finances.
By late 1993, most syndicated and nonsyndicated bank claims, 85 percent
of claims over $250,000 and all smaller claims had been resolved. Iran had
also received a $278 million payment for undelivered Iranian-owned,
American-made military equipment.

Since January 1984, Iran has occupied a spot on the U.S. State Department's list of countries that sponsor international terrorism. When he
designated Iran as a sponsor, Secretary of State George Shultz was reacting in part to the October 1983 bombing of U.S. Marine headquarters in
Beirut. The Reagan administration was also laying the legal basis to prevent U.S. equipment from helping Iran against Iraq. Subsequently, the
Arms Export Control Act prohibited foreign military sales and U.S. government consent "to any transfer of any munitions item" to Iran. Under
the Export Administration Act of 1979, sales of certain other goods and
technology was restricted through licensing requirements. By law, U.S.
representatives were also required to oppose international financial assis-

tance to Iran by voice and vote. The Foreign Assistance Act barred all aid to countries providing support for acts of international terrorism. These measures which all contain waiver provisions, form the basis of U.S. operational policy toward Iran as of early 1994.

The Reagan administration's policy toward Iran was two-faced. Officially the policy was to tilt increasingly in favor of Iraq since for most of the Iran-Iraq War the general expectation was that Iraq would lose and a triumphant Iran would present unacceptable threats to the Arabian peninsula and nearby countries. Consequently a tough international arms embargo against Iran was instigated (Operation Staunch) which denied Iran much-needed spare parts and weapons for the war.

Indeed, it was precisely the effectiveness of Operation Staunch that set the stage for the disastrous Iran-Contra affair concocted in the National Security Council during the second Reagan administration. The idea was to use Iran's desperate need for American arms, especially antitank and anti-air missiles, as the basis of a covert deal with the mullahs to release American hostages held in Lebanon. In exchange missiles were taken out of Israeli stocks and flown to Teheran. Some of the profits from these arms sales went to fund the American-backed Contra guerrillas in Nicaragua (whom Congress had barred from receiving U.S. aid).

In the aftermath of the Iran-Contra scandal and intensified U.S. military involvement in the Persian Gulf, President Reagan banned Iranian imports. He gave several justifications for this action, including unprovoked attacks on U.S. vessels, Iran's refusal to implement Security Council Resolution 598 calling for an end to the Iran-Iraq War, aggression against nonbelligerent nations of the Gulf and sponsorship of terrorism. Though subsequent amendments have slightly altered the original executive order, most Iranian imports remain prohibited from the United States. Oil sales whose proceeds are used to replenish the U.S.-Iran Claims Tribunal accounts were exempted from the order in 1991.

The U.S. Congress passed its most restrictive legislation against Iran in late 1992. In previous years, Congress had addressed the treatment of the Baha'i, other human rights abuses, the Iran-Iraq War, aid restrictions and other Iranian actions. The Iran-Iraq Arms Non-Proliferation Act of 1992, signed in October 1992, included a series of prohibitions and sanctions against violators. The act bars the Foreign Military Sales program, commercial arms sales, the transfer of restricted goods and technology as well as nuclear material and technology.

The act also institutes sanctions against individuals and private firms, foreign or American, and foreign governments that assist Iran or Iraq in acquiring weapons of mass destruction and their means of delivery (missiles). Sanctions also apply to anyone contributing to the "efforts by Iran and Iraq…to acquire destabilizing numbers and types of advanced conventional weapons." The president is able to waive the sanctions only if he determines that "it is essential to the national interest of the United States." Congress was deeply concerned about Iran's development of weapons of mass destruction and hoped that the act would undermine Iranian programs.

Finally, U.S. diplomatic efforts have tried to internationalize the U.S. government's attempt to keep various technologies from reaching Iran. Talks with representatives from the G-7 nations in November 1992 failed to bring about greater restrictions.[5] In June 1993, Secretary of State Warren Christopher pressed members of the European Community to block technology sales that could help Iran develop weapons of mass destruction. While the Europeans agreed to study the issue, they declined to impose new export limitations. Iran's growing economic problems, especially its apparent debt crisis, could cause tensions and disagreements between the United States, European states and Japan.[7]

IRAN'S GRIEVANCES TOWARD AMERICA

Knowing why the United States distrusts Iran tells only half the story. Americans need to understand why the Islamic regime expresses such anger against the United States and singles it out as the ultimate source of all its troubles. In a general sense, Iranian leaders believe that America refuses to accept the revolution and is unable to normalize relations with a country that embraces Islamic ideals.

Iran's grievances with America are also linked to key events from the past. First and foremost was U.S. support for the Pahlavi regime, a regime the revolutionaries have always considered both illegitimate and anti-clerical. Indifferent to the Shah's corruption and human rights abuses, the United States provided the Shah with arms, resources, financial aid and business access. The final insult to the new regime was the decision to allow the Shah to receive medical treatment for cancer in the United States in 1979 after his exile. This event was the catalyst for the takeover of the U.S. embassy in Teheran and the subsequent hostage crisis.

Another provocation stems from American support for Iraq during the 1980-88 war. The United States began to favor Iraq in 1982 after Iran had repelled the initial Iraqi offensive; Iranian forces were poised to cross the Shatt al-Arab and capture the Iraqi port of Basra, thereby threatening Kuwait and the Arab states of the Gulf. The United States launched Operation Staunch at a time when Iran desperately needed modern weapons. To the Iranians, who lost hundreds of thousands of lives during the eight-year war, the combined American policy of aiding Iraq and coordinating an arms embargo against Iranian military forces was irrefutable evidence of hostility.

In addition, toward the end of the Iran-Iraq War the U.S. Navy began to conduct military operations against Iranian maritime assets as part of its mission to protect oil tankers. The United States deployed about thirty naval vessels in the Persian Gulf, and in various incidents sank Iranian ships, destroyed oil platforms and captured or killed Iranian crew members. On July 3, 1988, an Iranian Airbus A-300 flying from Bandar Abbas to Dubai was shot down over the Gulf by a missile fired from the *U.S.S. Vincennes*. Two hundred and fifty Iranians were killed. Iran demanded compensation from the United States in the International Court of Justice.

Iranian leaders believe that the United States has spurned attempts at reconciliation since the end of the Iran-Iraq War. In their opinion they have made two major concessions—the release of hostages in Lebanon and their tacit cooperation with the allied efforts during Desert Storm. They resent never having been thanked or rewarded for such behavior. Acting on President Bush's January 1989 offer that "good will begets good will," Iran used its influence and paid money to secure the release of Western hostages in Lebanon. The United States failed to follow up with a positive response. Similarly, Iran was snubbed in the aftermath of Desert Storm when it was excluded from the postwar discussions on a Gulf security regime.

Further aggravating the Iranian regime, the United States still refuses to release Iranian assets impounded after the revolution. Iranian leaders see no reason why outstanding claims cannot be settled. Although many claims have been resolved, Iran focuses on the money in the Security and Interest Accounts and the unsettled claims relating to the Foreign Military Sales program. President Rafsanjani has said that the release of these assets, which could amount to billions of dollars for Iran, would go far to improve relations between the two countries. The United States disputes this claim, arguing that the claims outstanding are in the low millions, not billions.

Iran is also troubled by American policies designed to weaken the Iranian economy. Under Rafsanjani, Iran has accumulated large amounts of short and long-term debt. Loans from international financial institutions would help it meet debt payments and support its capital needs. However, U.S. antiterrorism laws require U.S. representatives to these institutions to oppose Iranian loan requests, impeding its access to credit. The Iranian economy is also hurt by the U.S. trade embargo and strict export controls on sales of technology to Iran. Moreover, the U.S. threat of sanctions against countries attempting to export sensitive technology to Iran could further limit Iran's trading partners. From the Iranian perspective, these policies unfairly hinder Iran's right to strengthen its economy. Iranian leaders perceive the United States as intent on undermining the revolution's political legitimacy by destabilizing the economy and impeding modernization.

U.S. military activity in the Gulf is also threatening to Iran. Aside from the continued presence of American armed forces, Iran is disturbed by large-scale U.S. arms transfers to the region and U.S. security agreements with GCC countries. The United States has transferred billions of dollars worth of weaponry to Kuwait, Saudi Arabia and other Gulf states.

Finally, the Iranian government bitterly resents the Western media's reliance on opponents of the regime as sources for negative press and television coverage. They argue that the People's Mojahedin and other exiled groups constantly fan the flames of anti-Iranian sentiment by unjustly and inaccurately depicting the Iranian threat, including the allegations concerning an Iranian nuclear program.

THE LEGACY OF PAST RELATIONS

As long as this bitter legacy conditions day-to-day thinking in both countries, any meaningful dialogue is unlikely except perhaps on an ad hoc basis with specific issues that require immediate attention. If, however, both countries were prepared to begin discussions about ways to overcome current problems without endlessly regressing to past stances, progress might be possible. By all indications such an approach was adopted by Israeli and Palestinian negotiators in the secret Oslo talks that produced the breakthrough in that relationship. Both parties were acutely aware that if they dwelt on the past, nothing would resolved and the talks would break down in acrimony. This lesson is worth digesting and should be taken to heart by American negotiators if and when Iran is capable of sitting down at the table.

IRAN'S DOMESTIC PROBLEMS

Iran's grievances with the United States come at a time when the country is experiencing profound political and economic distress, conditions that are likely to fuel more domestic instability.[1] The mullahs' reaction to increased instability is unpredictable. Will they be more pragmatic or confrontational? In extremis, could the regime fall? What is clear is that a power struggle between President Rafsanjani and his conservative opponents led by Supreme Religious Leader Ayatollah Khamenei continues against a backdrop of growing domestic discontent, economic weakness and volatile international relations.

INTERNAL CONFUSION AND WEAKNESSES

In 1992, Iran experienced the worst urban riots since the revolution. The government's attempts to evict squatters in major cities backfired as thousands of frustrated, impoverished Iranians took to the streets. In Teheran, Meshed, Arak, Shiraz and Khorramabad, rioters attacked police, burned cars and buildings and tried to reclaim their shelters. The rampage of looting and burning put the Iranian government on notice that the expectations of many poor Iranians have not been met, even as the government blamed the riots on a foreign conspiracy. For the general populace low wages, rampant inflation, rising prices, insufficient housing and unemployment are daily reminders of Iran's economic disarray. Nostalgia is widespread for the old days when the Shah reigned, the mullahs were quiescent and America was a friend rather than the Great Satan. The remaining revolutionaries find such attitudes extremely threatening; like Khomeini, they are well aware of the seductive appeal of American and Western lifestyles, culture and ethos.

The Iranian regime is weak because of two, mutually reinforcing conditions. Its leadership is bitterly divided and its economy for the past fifteen years has been devastated by revolution, a catastrophic war, chronic mismanagement and corruption, Western sanctions, oil market fluctuations, diplomatic isolation and natural disasters. Foreign exchange earnings from increased oil sales are not sufficient to sustain both rearmament and the economic growth necessary to keep pace with the rise in population and deferred consumer expectations. Without better economic results, Iran will be unable to manage the political, military and demographic challenges of the coming years. The economy must recover not only from war but from the damage of Khomeini's statist policies which undermined the business and merchant classes through intimidation and confiscation of property. Like Eastern Europe, the Soviet Union and India, Iran has learned the hard way that state control is an ineffective economic model for a developing country. Rafsanjani has done an about-face and adopted the Shah's prerevolutionary economic strategy. This includes marketization and privatization; attempts to increase oil production (this was considered treason in 1979 but production is now sustainable at 3.5 million barrels a day and could surge to 4 million barrels a day for short periods); a five-year plan that calls for industry to increase faster than any other sector; and a desire to woo foreign investment, removing some restrictions and going beyond the policy of the Shah, when the share of foreign ownership was held to 49 percent. The leadership hopes that a strategy based on marketization and privatization will bring about wage and price decontrol, lower subsidies and an increase in Iran's ability to attract foreign private investment, including management, technology and capital. One aspect of the strategy, the final unification of the exchange rate, proceeded as planned in late March 1993.

There are a few positive indicators in today's Iranian economy. Agriculture is growing—though not as fast as under the Shah—and improvements are being made in infrastructure, roads and electrification. Some industrial projects, many dating from the Shah's time, have been completed. However, most other indicators remain negative. The gross domestic product (GDP) is still near the 1978-79 level in real terms. Unemployment is 14 to 15 percent (though some private sources put it is as high as 30 percent). Inflation is 18 percent (while some private sources suggest even higher figures of 30 to 50 percent). The balance of payments has been in the red for ten of the last fourteen years and the government has had a budget deficit every year for the past fourteen years.[2]

To try to correct some of these problems, Iran is intent on increasing oil exports, petroleum production and gas exports. Nonoil exports, especially industrial ones, are also rising. In this regard, the continuing U.N. sanctions against Iraq are a blessing for Iran. The nightmare haunting Iranian planners is that Iraq may eventually resume full-scale oil production, further depressing prices and reducing Iran's foreign exchange earnings.

The international economic environment remains unfriendly. The United States and, to a lesser extent, the European Union and Japan are avoiding trade and investment relationships with Iran. The GCC and Iran maintain formal but tenuous economic relations. Iran hopes for profitable economic relations with Central Asia and retains friendly and cooperative ties with much of the Third World. However, neither Central Asia nor other markets in developing countries can provide enough short-term stimulus to lift Iran from its economic difficulties.

Against this background of economic weakness, the leadership struggle in Teheran has intensified. After a number of early successes, President Rafsanjani's political power has been undermined. In the Majles elections of April 1992, Rafsanjani engineered the exclusion of radical candidates by declaring them unqualified to run; many other radicals were defeated in the actual voting process. These developments were rightly interpreted as the triumph of pragmatists over radicals. As a result, Rafsanjani was able to reduce the legislative power of the radicals in the Majles.

Despite their election losses, the radicals retain strong bases of support in the Revolutionary Guard, the internal security apparatus and various revolutionary institutions.[3] The radicals fear the return of the Western-educated intelligentsia from exile. They have therefore mounted a campaign against Western dress, permissiveness and the arts. They fear that their children, the true heirs of the revolution, will eventually be denied places at the universities and in government.

The radicals' campaign prompted the forced resignation in mid-1992 of the Minister of Culture and Islamic Guidance, Muhammad Khatami, whose permissiveness in artistic expression was seen as a sign of the return of Western-influenced ideas and culture. Supreme Religious Leader Khamenei further warned that the "fifth column" would destroy Iran from within. Fear of losing control prompted socially conservative radicals to demand the reassertion of and support for Islamic movements. This resurgence of militancy with its concomitant anti-Western and anti-American rhetoric dates back to the death of Ayatollah Khomeini in 1989, which precipitated a crisis in the spiritual leadership of the country and an opening for more divisive politics. Khamenei, who constitutionally has only assumed Khomeini's spiritual mantle, has failed to fulfill the role of spiritual leader in a similar manner as Khomeini because his religious credentials are not accepted by more senior clerics. To legitimize his position as the leader of the Islamic community, and to cover for his lack of seniority, Khamenei has taken tough stances on aiding Muslims in Bosnia and the Israeli-occupied territories. The issue of religious leadership has become a source of extremist rhetoric and conflict and helps account for Iran's greater ideological assertiveness abroad, especially in Bosnia, Sudan, the West Bank and Gaza.

Inevitably much of the in-fighting among the leadership concerns personal power. Influential clerics will not willingly give up their fiefdoms that control large amounts of foreign exchange, sell goods and make huge purchases abroad. Potential investors are put off by the bureaucratic red tape and the possibility of another round of confiscations. Corruption is widespread, creating uncertainty and undermining public and business confidence. Corruption has always existed in modern Iran but in the past, businesses were able to rely on a predictable system of payoffs and kick-backs. Today the declining economy has prompted more Iranian officials and intermediaries to demand compensation for helping in the bureau-cratic process. Along with heightened demand goes greater uncertainty; in short, even corruption no longer seems to work!

Another contentious issue concerns money given to spiritual leaders. Money affords them leverage and therefore significant power. The seri-ousness of the issue was underscored by Khamenei who, in an attempt to curtail other cleric's political clout, requested that all alms donations be given in his name. The amount of money was not the key factor, rather, Khamenei was trying to deny his rivals the power of dispensing funds.[4]

Rafsanjani not only faces problems with the radicals opposed to the free market and privatization but centrists now blame him for the "struc-tural" problems of the Iranian economy and his inability to "deliver" ma-terial benefits to the population. Rafsanjani's desire to relax the rigid po-litical process has also created problems by making more public the dis-agreements about policy. In Iran, there is a lively media and the Majles is a genuine forum for debate about national issues (unlike in Iraq or Syria). However, this openness should not be confused with a free political *system*. Politics in Iran are conducted by an elite—and there is no evi-dence of any intention to open up the process to wider participation. In this area, Rafsanjani's problems are not unique. Other leaders in the Mid-dle East and beyond have been faced with a similar dilemma: how to be more open politically without exposing ills in the society, especially cor-ruption and human rights abuses.

While Rafsanjani was easily re-elected in the June 1993 presidential elections, many observers saw the results as a sign of his faltering support. Rafsanjani's share of the vote dropped from nearly 95 percent in 1989 to just over 63 percent. With little campaigning, the top challenger received 24 percent of the vote. Voter turnout also fell from 70 percent to 56 per-cent. The election results were widely viewed as signs of frustration and economic discontent; there was no mandate for Rafsanjani.[5]

Rafsanjani's disappointments were compounded when the Majles re-jected his choice for finance minister. Though Mohsen Nurbakhsh had served in the same position in the previous cabinet, the August 1993 vote to confirm him fell short. Some saw conservative deputies defending the interests of the wealthy merchants in sacking Nurbakhsh. Others suggest-ed that this was a warning to Rafsanjani in regard to his attempts to at-tract foreign investment and build a free-market economy.[6]

IMPACT ON FOREIGN POLICY

Iran's leadership rivalries have resulted in incoherence in Iranian foreign policy. Because no single leader or core group is in charge, policies appear haphazard and inconsistent, the consequence of competing forces asserting dominance in particular areas. A classic episode took place in the summer of 1992. Despite unresolved differences caused by the Rushdie affair, British and Iranian officials had been negotiating a more open relationship which included greater cultural exchanges. At the same time, two employees of the Iranian embassy in London and an Iranian student were caught by British authorities planning further action against Salman Rushdie. As a result, relations between the two countries soured all the more and Britain invoked much tougher policies against Iran. This is not the only example of Iran's mysterious and chaotic foreign policy decision-making, but it is representative of the problem the regime faces.

Fiscal pressures also put constraints on Iranian foreign policy. Beset by a growing economic crisis, Iran lacks the funds for a high profile activist, interventionist foreign policy. For example, Iran's hope of becoming a key player in Central Asia depends much more on strong economic relations than on the ideological appeal of the Islamic state. The rearmament program will be hampered by a shortage of resources at home. Key arms suppliers, especially the cash-starved Russians, are looking for hard currency. They are unlikely to agree to deferred payments or credit agreements. (Yet if the Iranian government chooses to spend scarce resources on the military, this will further jeopardize the improvement of the economy.)

On the other hand, economic problems at home could increase the likelihood of a military encounter with a neighboring state as a diversionary tactic. Under extreme circumstances, a well-planned resource grab against a rich, weak Arab state similar to what Saddam Hussein attempted against Kuwait in August 1990 might be seen to have positive economic benefits. Had Saddam Hussein been more imaginative and less crude and compulsive over Kuwait, he could have procured his extra income without resorting to massive force and ensuring the enmity of the world.

One possible scenario of Iranian military adventurism concerns the dispute over the Qatari North Field gas dome. While Iran claims some 30 percent of the dome, Qatar places the figure near 5 percent. It is doubtful whether Iran will receive even that much. When the dome comes into production in 1997, it will be an immense revenue source. With the issue of ownership rights already in dispute, Iranian military intervention with the goal of ameliorating its financial troubles is not unthinkable.[7]

The more probable outcome, however, is that military adventurism would merely add to Iran's economic troubles. True, military excursions could become a tool of the leadership rivalry as one faction seeks to position itself or prove a certain level of toughness vis-a-vis another. Military diversions may even be used to legitimize the revolution and help facilitate the spread of Iranian ideology. But, it is precisely this possibility of Iranian military activity that intensifies the fears of its neighbors and strengthens their determination to keep an American commitment to their defense.

IRAN AND ITS NEIGHBORS

Iran's domestic woes are set against a backdrop of remarkable changes in the international environment. After nearly two centuries of domination by major foreign powers, the Middle East is no longer the battleground for competitions among outside actors with vastly stronger capabilities than the regional powers. In theory, Iran and other local states should now be able to exercise more initiative and find ways to determine their own destinies. As with the rest of the international community, the Cold War had helped shape Iranian foreign policy and alliances. The breakup of the Soviet empire has brought Central Asia and the Caucasus back within the sphere of the historical Middle East. Potentially, Iran has new arenas for its ideology and new economic markets. The temporary eclipse of Iraq's regional clout has further enhanced this opportunity. However, in reality, a review of Iran's relations with its neighbors reveals much ambiguity among the parties with mutual insecurity being the dominant theme.

IMPACT OF THE NEW WORLD ORDER

Despite a changed world, Iran still finds itself operating in a hostile international environment. The new order is dominated by the United States, which poses a particularly troublesome challenge to the Iranian revolution. In addition, ethnic and religious minorities, hostile regimes, wars and chaos surround Iran. It is not difficult, in other words, to see why *any* regime in Teheran would feel insecure in this particular neighborhood.

America's preeminent position in the Middle East is the key threat to the Iranian regime. Given Iran's preoccupation with America and its leaders' penchant for conspiracy theories, it is hardly surprising that the regime feels threatened. It was not only awed by the speed and ruthlessness with which American-led military forces destroyed Saddam Hussein's war machine (in contrast to Iran's humiliating and costly defeat) but the fact that in the *aftermath* of Desert Storm the U.S. presence remains very visible. The key Arab Gulf states now have more formal bilateral military relations with the United States and are expanding military cooperation with each other as well as building up their own arsenals. The United States is the predominant military power in the Persian Gulf; Iran's archenemy occupies both the global and the regional driver's seat.

Similarly, the redrawing of the Middle East map has created new and fluid frontier zones to Iran's west, north and east that pose challenges at the same time as they create opportunities. The defeat of Iraq during Desert Storm left the central Iraqi government at odds with Iraqi Kurds and Shiites. While the breakup of Iraq is unlikely, the overall instability of the region could undermine any Iranian advantages gained from a weaker Iraqi government and military. The conflict between Armenia and Azerbaijan and the links between independent Azerbaijan and Iranian Azerbaijan are just two of the many regional issues that now have direct consequences for Iran. As for Central Asia, it is not clear that Iran will have any significant influence in the new republics. A host of countries—Russia, the United States, Turkey, Saudi Arabia, Pakistan, China, India and even South Korea and Israel—have opportunities to play roles there that will likely prevent Iran from assuming a dominant position among foreign players.

The end of the Cold War has also had an impact on constellations in the broader international political arena. Iranian leaders can no longer seek protection or support from familiar multilateral groupings and organizations that tended to band together in international forums. The Non-Aligned Movement no longer exists; the Islamic axis is in disarray and its resurrection is unlikely in view of the many conflicts within the Muslim world itself. Even the term "Third World" seems increasingly archaic and irrelevant to the new regional dynamics emerging in South and East Asia, as well as in the Middle East itself.

RELATIONS WITH SYRIA: PERMANENT OR EPHEMERAL ALLIES?

Syria remains the key Middle East country with which Iran continues to maintain good relations. This alliance evolved in the 1980s, in part because of mutual fears of Saddam Hussein's Iraq, but also because of the common goal of confronting Israel and the United States. However, the end of the Cold War and Syria's dramatic reappraisal of its role in the Arab-Israeli peace process has cast a shadow over the enduring qualities of the Teheran-Damascus axis. Both countries continue to collaborate in supporting the virulently anti-Israel Hizbollah organization in Lebanon, and Syria continues to allow weapons to be shipped from Iran to Lebanon. However, if Israel and Syria reach an accord leading to peaceful relations, an end to all violent activity by Hizbollah and Iran's role as arms supplier will surely be part of the agreement. Syria would also be under great pressure to refrain from further cooperation with Iran on weapons developments and arms transfers. The result would be to significantly weaken Iran and force its leaders to rethink their strategy towards the Arab world and Iran's role as leader of the rejectionist front.

On the other hand, if the peace process collapses, Syria and Iran are capable of strengthening the power of the rejectionists who could increase military cooperation including mutual transfers of advanced weapons systems such as surface-to-surface missiles. This, in turn, could exacerbate strategic relations with Israel and intensify the overall regional arms race.[1] It could also increase the likelihood of an informal alliance to deny the Kurds the possibility of an autonomous region.

RELATIONS WITH IRAQ: WHY SADDAM HUSSEIN SERVES IRANIAN INTERESTS

Hostility between Iran and Iraq was a prominent feature of Cold War politics in the 1970s and 1980s. Although alliances shifted, Iraq served as a counterweight to Iranian designs in the Gulf region. Both countries constantly competed for military superiority. In 1972, Iraq and the Soviet Union signed a treaty of friendship at a time when U.S.-Iranian relations were strong. The 1979 Iranian revolution and the outbreak of the Iran-Iraq War in 1980 upended allegiances as the virulently anti-Western Iranian regime publicly rejected the United States, which, in turn, soon began to tilt in favor of Iraq. Both Soviet and American officials believed, at different times, that strengthening Iraq helped curb Iranian regional ambitions. With its military defeat in 1991, Iraq is currently unable to fulfill this role. Now a pariah with an economy in shambles, Iraq's vast oil resources lie underutilized as international ostracism continues. While Iraq is not permanently sidelined, the coming years do not bode well for Saddam Hussein's regime unless he can persuade the United Nations to lift the sanctions on Iraqi oil sales.

In addition, Iraq no longer commands the support of Russia, which has expressed no interest in serving as Iraq's patron as long as Saddam Hussein remains in power. This does not bar Iraq from courting other potential patrons like China or buying weapons on the well-stocked open market. Yet these approaches will take time. Without a great power rivalry, the replenishment of Iraqi weaponry is a more difficult task, though once it resumes major oil exports, its market could become very attractive to a host of arms suppliers, including Russia, China and Eastern Europe.

A weak Iraq leaves Iran in a stronger military and economic position. However, the fact that the Islamic regime has chosen to antagonize its Arab Gulf neighbors, who themselves are fearful of Iraq, is a sure sign that the regime has a divided, inconsistent foreign policy. Iran is unable to fully exploit its natural geopolitical advantages and the plight of its most dangerous regional rival. However, if its leaders can agree on a single foreign policy and overcome the country's severe economic crisis, Iran is capable, by dint of geography, population and ambition, of exercising considerable power and influence over the Persian Gulf region. Whether this represents a "hegemonic aspiration" is a matter for debate, but much will depend on how politically secure the conservative Arab

Gulf states are and the extent to which the American presence in the region deters or spurs Iranian ambitions.

Could Iran and Iraq ever patch up their differences to the point of cooperating with each other against the American-led opposition? While there are undoubtedly some areas where both countries work together, especially in sales of limited quantities of smuggled Iraqi oil, Iran has much to lose if it connives in the rehabilitation of Saddam Hussein. Its leaders must know Saddam's track record. If rehabilitated, it will mean sanctions will be lifted and Iraq will once more be able to use its money to buy weapons and intimidate neighbors. Given its smaller population and huge untapped oil reserves, Iraq would be able to devote a greater percentage of its revenues to military expenditure than Iran. This would not only pose a major threat to the region, but since Saddam Hussein is likely to be in a hurry to seek revenge for his Gulf War humiliations, Iraqi oil would flood the market, further depressing oil prices, which, in turn, would have a profoundly negative impact on the Iranian economy.

On the other hand, if Saddam Hussein were replaced by a less tainted but nevertheless nationalist and anti-Western leader, a rapprochement with Teheran might be conceivable. If the new Iraqi leadership were able to quickly persuade the international community to lift sanctions, Iran might calculate that it would be to its advantage to establish good relations rather than be seen as the enemy. In turn, the Iraqis might find it useful to satisfy Iranian demands on issues such as the status of the Iranian opposition forces currently stationed in Iraq. Both countries might find common ground in efforts to deny the Kurds greater autonomy and certainly both sides would want to challenge American military domination and the international efforts to deny both countries advanced armaments.

RUSSIA: COOPERATING WITH TEHERAN

Iran's relations with Russia are multifaceted and lack the zero-sum quality of the U.S.-Iranian confrontation. Because of Iran's location on the periphery of the former Soviet empire and Russia's historic suspicion of Turkey, Russian leaders hope that by promoting and expanding political and economic ties with the Islamic Republic, they will help to maintain stability in Central Asia, avoid the spread of radical Islam and stimulate trade and commercial cooperation.

Russia is threatened by unrest around its periphery. Conflict and turmoil in Georgia, Armenia, Azerbaijan, Tajikistan and Afghanistan contribute to regional instability and undermine Russian efforts to secure its new borders, protect Russian minorities in the former republics and promote economic ties. Russia believes that stability is also in Iran's basic interest. Teheran fears that the crisis in Azerbaijan may engulf the approximately 15 million Azeris living in Iran. Both sides hope Russo-Iranian cooperation will help contain the crisis. Meanwhile, Iran needs arms and seeks inclusion in Central Asian and Gulf politics. Both Russia and Iran believe they can benefit from strong and stable bilateral relations.

Yet even as some Russians advocate a closer relationship with Iran, Russian fears of Islamic fundamentalism are genuine and, under certain circumstances, could weaken the Iranian connection. If confrontation between Iran and the Gulf Arabs — with whom Russia has good relations — intensifies, Russia may be forced to side with Iran on the one hand or the United States and Arab Gulf states on the other. Considering the importance of its relations with the United States and the financial pull of the Gulf states, Iran would likely come in a distant second.

The issue is further complicated by Iran's role in the Afghan civil war, its interests in the Azerbaijani-Armenian conflict, its rearmament program and its opposition to the Arab-Israeli peace process, which Russia cosponsors. Because of the diversity of Islamic groups in Central Asia and the restraint Iran has shown so far in keeping out of the conflicts, Russia does not fear Iranian domination or subversion. Russia would like to assume that the two countries are not pursuing conflicting objectives.

The Russian dilemma on arms sales and the peace process raises another set of issues. Russian-Iranian cooperation in the military arena has led to several major arms sales, particularly since 1989. Russia holds that its military cooperation with Iran is based on the principles set forth in the talks on conventional arms sales initiated by the permanent five members of the U.N. Security Council (the P-5) and that the weapons will only be sold for self-defense. These arms exports are so important to the Russian economy that even the most pro-Western Russian leader could not afford to turn down this opportunity. This indicates that Moscow might be willing to alienate Washington if that were the price to continue unhampered arms sales to Teheran. On the other hand, Russia takes its cosponsorship of the Arab-Israeli peace process seriously and would like a greater role in the future. This will inevitably lead to further friction with Iran, given Iran's vehement opposition to the Madrid process. Russia would not take kindly to Iranian action that undermines one of the few Middle East issues in which Russia has some influence. Russia would like to see a better U.S.-Iranian relationship, with all parties participating in Gulf security. Moscow does not want to be cut out of the Middle East but it is increasingly reluctant to have Washington dictate the terms of engagement.

Strengthened ties between Iran and Russia are a double-edged sword and confront the United States with a profound dilemma. On the one hand, a warmer relationship between the two states will lead to increased arms and technology transfers to a government Washington considers hostile. Moreover, if Iranian-Russian cooperation on nuclear projects continues, it will heighten the potential for nuclear proliferation. On the other hand, Russia might exercise a moderating influence on the revolutionary regime and could function as a mediator between Iran and the West. A political communique initialed by Moscow and Teheran in March 1993 states that neither will use force against the other and, more importantly for the United States, will not use force against countries one of the partners deems friendly.[3] Thus, by maintaining healthy ties with Moscow, Washington can try to influence Iran indirectly while the danger of Iranian military adventurism remains limited.

It remains to be seen whether the new constellation of political forces in Russia following the December 1993 elections will significantly change Russian policy toward Iran. On the one hand, the more nationalist mood in Moscow is likely to strengthen the arguments of those who believe Russia has been too subservient to American interests in the Middle East and thereby denied itself lucrative economic deals, including more arms sales to countries such as Iran. On the other hand, if the dominant personality in the new Russian parliament is Vladimir Zhirinovosky, whose far right party won nearly 25 percent of the vote, both Iran and the United States may be losers. Zhirinovosky is an old Middle East hand and has recently published a book outlining his geopolitical views on the region. Entitled *The Last Thrust Southward*, the book describes Turkey, Iran and Afghanistan as enemies of Russia. Russia needs to subjugate these countries and reabsorb lost territories of the Caucasus and Central Asia if it is to fulfill its destiny and gain permanent access to the warm water ports in the Mediterranean Sea and Indian Ocean. Iraq, especially Saddam Hussein, is seen as the natural ally of Russia under this scenario.[4]

TURKEY: COOPERATION OR COMPETITION IN THE CAUCASUS AND CENTRAL ASIA?

The end of the Cold War and the 1991 Persian Gulf War have refocused Turkish interests in Asia. With the Soviet threat diminished under Gorbachev, Turkey was willing and able to assume a central role in the allied coalition against Iraq. Although Turkey's assertiveness in regional politics carries prestige, its redefined position has created tension with Iran even though both countries are members of the Economic Cooperation Organization.[5] Although relations improved in 1992 when Turkey's prime minister, Suleyman Demirel, visited Teheran in September and October and signed agreements covering political, economic and cultural areas, relations during 1993 became strained.[6]

Both Iran and Turkey are interested in gaining influence in the Central Asian and Transcaucasian republics and both countries have signed agreements with these fledgling countries.[7] Observers differ sharply on the impact that the Turco-Iranian relationship may have on these republics. One school argues that greater competition will ensue between the two opposing models of political development for the Turco-Muslim peoples of Central Asia and the Caucasus: the secular democratic model of Turkey and the Islamic model projected by Iran. The other school considers this an oversimplification and maintains that options for the new republics cannot be reduced to these terms. It portrays the supposed Iran-Turkish rivalry as a Western creation that exaggerates the potential influence of the two states on the region.

Yet both Iran and Turkey have penetrated the republics on cultural and ideological levels and remain at loggerheads over many important issues. Turkey's secularism reflects its aversion to Islamic fundamentalism as symbolized by Iran. This rejection coalesced after the journalist Ugur Mumcu, a prosecular writer highly critical of the actions of Islamic fundamentalists, was assassinated on January 24, 1993. At the funeral thousands of Turks chanted: "Turkey will never be Iran."[8] The government arrested members of Islamic Action, an Islamic fundamentalist group with alleged ties to Iran.[9]

Another dimension of Iranian-Turkish relations is the Kurdish issue. Ties are strained by the activities of the Kurdish Workers' Party (PKK). When Kurdish terrorists stepped up violence inside Turkey, Prime Minister Demirel accused Iran of supporting them.[10] Turkey is also alarmed by the separatist tendencies of its Kurdish population and harbors concerns that Teheran is playing this card to exert pressure on Ankara. Regional states realize that the Kurdish issue is a loose cannon that Iran can manipulate by funneling arms to Kurdish movements in Turkey. On the other hand, the Kurdish issue may yet prove to be a catalyst for Turco-Iranian cooperation. Profound regional fears of fragmentation and balkanization could compel Turkey, Iran, Iraq and Syria to come together in dealing with the problem. Governments may see such coordination as the only way to preserve the territorial integrity of those states hosting large numbers of Kurds.

Aside from these more obvious disputes, the two countries have been engaged in diplomatic maneuvers over the conflict between Armenia and

Azerbaijan. Although it values its ties with the Muslim Azerbaijanis, Iran has sent signals that closer relations with Armenia might limit Turkish influence in the region. In December 1992, Vice-President Gagik Aru-tyunyan of Armenia visited Teheran, and both sides characterized their deliberations as a breakthrough in Armenian-Iranian cooperation. More important, Iran and Armenia are considering signing an agreement that would make energy-starved Armenia dependent on Iran for much of its natural gas needs.[11] Ankara feels slighted because it also made advances to Armenia: In November 1992 with strong American pressure, Turkey and Armenia signed an agreement on electric power, but reactions from Turkish opposition parties and Azerbaijan quickly stalled the deal.[12] (They accused the Turkish government of selling out and betraying its historic ties to the Azeris.) There was little doubt that Ankara's motive in dealing with Armenia was to try and head off Iran. Making the situation all the more volatile, senior Russian officials have urged Armenia to develop relations with Iran in order to stymie Turkish influence in the region.[13]

However, recent Armenian military advances in Azerbaijan have created new security dilemmas for Iran. The actual fighting has edged closer to Iran, with Azeri cities outside Nagorno-Karabakh coming under Armenian control. In addition, hundreds of thousands of refugees have fled the expanding zone of conflict. Many refugees head for the Aras River, part of the border between Iran and Azerbaijan. Such growing instability heightens pressures on Iran. In August, 1993, an Iranian foreign ministry statement "seriously warn[ed] the Armenian forces for their repeated aggressions" close to Iran's borders.[14]

Turkey is suspicious of Iran and believes it is aspiring to a position as a regional power. It fears that this desire to influence extends beyond the cultural and ideological realms to the political. While Ankara does not currently perceive Iran as a military threat, it is alarmed by Iran's support of terrorist elements within Turkey. To show its displeasure, in February 1993, Turkey joined twelve other nations and voted to suspend Export-Import Bank guarantees for exports to Iran. In response Iranian Foreign Minister Velayati warned that Iran would take revenge on "a clearly hostile policy" pursued by Ankara.[15]

RELATIONS WITH AFGHANISTAN

Since the communist Najibullah regime fell in April 1992, the situation in Afghanistan has degenerated into a violent conflict among factions of the Mujahedeen. Iran's policies in the Afghan conflict are as complex as the quagmire itself, reflecting internal tensions in Iran, Iran's power struggles with Arab states, suspicions of the former Soviet Union and its desire to avoid becoming too embroiled in this endless conflict. Traditionally, Iran's main goal in Afghanistan was to protect the Shiite minority, approximately 25 percent of the population in Afghanistan. Iran backed the Hizb il-Wahdat, a Shiite Muslim militia force primarily composed of ethnic Hazara fighters. The Shiite Hazaras are concentrated in western Afghanistan near the border with Iran.

In April and May 1992, Iran began praising Ahmad Shah Masood, the head of Jamiat Islami faction, for his efforts to avert a bloodbath in Kabul. President Rafsanjani initiated the opening because of Iran's geopolitical interests in improving ties to Tajikistan—a springboard for consolidating influence in Central Asia. Iran believed that the more secular Masood, a Tajik, had closer ties to the former communists in the government of Tajikistan. Islamic fundamentalist Gulbuddin Hekmatyar, leader of Hizb Islami, on the other hand, worries the government of Tajikistan. Iran also began to see Hekmatyar as the proxy of the Sunni Arab elements in the region. Hard-liners in Iran, though, were not so enthralled and feared that Masood and Afghani President Burhanuddin Rabbani, also a Tajik, would steer Afghanistan away from an Iranian-style Islamic republic.

The situation in Afghanistan degenerated into outright factional warfare in mid-1992. By September, Afghanistan was ruled by several distinct armed groups. The government, led by President Rabbani and members of Jamiat Islami, remained in Kabul with some support from Tajiks in the north. Gen. Rashid Dostam, an Uzbek and former leader of forces under ex-President Najibullah, used his powerful militia to back the government in Kabul while simultaneously exploring the possibility of a secular, autonomous Uzbek state in the north. In the west, Shiites in Hizb il-Wahdat clashed with Sunni (Wahabi) Muslims of Ittehad Islami. The greatest challenge to the government came from Hekmatyar's Hizb Islami, a mostly Pashtun force which is strongest in eastern and southern Afghanistan and the outskirts of Kabul.

Iran is not the only regional state with a stake in the war's outcome. Pakistan, Uzbekistan, Tajikistan and Saudi Arabia also support different factions in the ongoing struggle. Pakistan, a long-time supporter of Hekmatyar, is afraid of ethnic fragmentation that might incite the Pashtuns in Pakistan to rebel. Hekmatyar's vision of an Islamic fundamentalist state in Afghanistan allays these fears while also appeasing Islamic fundamentalist interests within Pakistan. Uzbekistan and Tajikistan, states with large numbers of ethnic kin in Afghanistan, are both ruled by secular governments opposed to militant Islamic forces in Afghanistan who, among other sins, provide arms and support for Tajikistan's Islamic opposition. Both countries support General Dostam's Uzbek militia. Saudi Arabia has consistently supported the Ittehad Islami, composed of fellow Wahabi Muslims. While the general tendencies of external powers are clear, confusing and contradictory allegations repeatedly surface. For example, over the many years of fighting reports have suggested that Iran, Pakistan and Saudi Arabia have all at various times established and cut off ties with Hekmatyar. Further complicating matters, many smaller groups and militias compete for power and control.

Iran sees several other opportunities in Afghanistan as well. A powerful Shiite force or Shiite autonomous zone would give Iran a foothold in Afghanistan. At the same time, such support helps counter the possibility of a Saudi-sponsored Sunni force or Hekmatyar-led region sympathetic to Arab states. Even if Iran's route to prosperity in Central Asia does not depend on the Tajiks or Uzbeks in Afghanistan, Iran may still find a way to benefit from the linkage between Afghanistan and the states to the north.

Many of these issues remain unsettled as Afghanistan continues to be ravaged by civil war. The periodic cease-fire agreements have fallen victim to renewed eruptions of hostilities, and this pattern seems likely to persist. Some observers had placed particular hopes on a cease-fire agreement brokered by Iran, Saudi Arabia and Pakistan and signed by six of the eight leading Mujahedeen factions on March 7, 1993. The accord brought Hekmatyar into the government as prime minister with Rabbani holding onto the presidency. But the fratricidal fighting went on and soon Hekmatyar was prime minister in name only. Forcibly barred from Kabul by Masood, Hekmatyar has formed his administration in Jalalabad, some 110 kilometers (68 miles) away from the capital, thereby creating a de facto rival government. Afghanistan is increasingly disintegrating into fiefdoms run by the various Mujahedeen leaders. In this chaotic climate it is unlikely that Iran's ties to Afghanistan are among its key political and diplomatic assets and that it will be prepared to commit major resources to further its interests.

THE CENTRAL ASIAN REPUBLICS: ECONOMIC VERSUS IDEOLOGICAL INTERESTS

Iran's geography makes the new Central Asian republics natural trading partners even though the republics are poor and their governments weak. Iran has already offered to serve as a road, rail and pipeline link for Central Asia to the Persian Gulf and beyond. The ethnic and religious distinctions, between Sunni and Shiite, Persian and Turkic, provide common ground in some cases and the basis for disagreement in others. Yet from the Iranian perspective, the broader Muslim dimension has obvious appeal. While critics suggest more sinister motives and see further plans for Iranian expansionism, good relations with the Central Asian countries would provide a welcome respite to an often isolated Iran.

To what extent is Iran in competition with Russia, Turkey, Pakistan and others for access and influence in these regions? For the foreseeable future the most important external power in Central Asia will be Russia. One leading historian has speculated not only that Russia will not abandon its interest in Central Asia but that its influence will be more pervasive than France's impact on its former African colonies.[16] Turkey has consistently demonstrated interest in the region and claims kinship with the Turkic people of Central Asia. Yet in spite of rhetoric to the contrary, Turkey's geography, the continued conflict in Azerbaijan and Armenia, the inability of its economy to support extensive foreign programs and its preoccupation with Kurdish issues pose great obstacles to significant Turkish involvement. Likewise Pakistani access to Central Asia is held hostage to the situation in Afghanistan. Although Russia will inevitably play a large role, the Central Asians are seeking to diversify their contacts and begin a process that will broaden their economic relationships over the long term. Thus even a powerful Russia will not be the sole player if the Central Asians have any say in the matter. The United States, Israel and Asian countries (ranging from China, which borders Kazakhstan and Kyrgyzstan, to the wealthier South Korea and Japan) have initiated economic contacts but appear uninterested in a cultural or political role.

With a prime geographic location, Iran could play an important role in Central Asia and the Caucasus. However, Iran's rhetoric will remain ahead of the reality and the Iranian presence is likely to increase very slowly. (See Appendix I for details on geography and logistics.)

Many argue that the threat of Iran's formulating a fundamentalist revolt in Central Asia is exaggerated. Some of Russia's Central Asian specialists have commended Iran's recent behavior in the region. In their view, Iran has shown remarkable restraint and has not exploited its influence inappropriately. The Tajik civil war is a case in point. Iran refrained from interfering, knowing full well that intervention would generate a negative Russian reaction. On the whole, these specialists believe Iran has been pragmatic and sensible in its policies towards Central Asia since the collapse of the Soviet Union.[17]

If Iran and its neighbors, including Turkey and Pakistan, develop strong economic ties and construct an infrastructure to help Central Asian countries export oil and natural gas, it would not necessarily run contrary to Western interests. It could lead to the economic development of a region that is of marginal importance to the United States and would bring more oil and gas onto the world market, thereby lowering prices. If Iran used such access to try to control oil prices it would be a dangerous development. But this would surely defeat the purpose of its economic ties with the region, since once Iran interfered with the market forces, Central Asian states would seek alternative access routes.

As far as radical Islam and Central Asia are concerned, apart from close Iranian religious and cultural ties with Tajikistan, there seems little likelihood that the Iranian model for a clerical and Islamic regime based on the Shiite religion has much appeal in Turkmenistan, Kazakhstan and Kyrgyzstan. There may be opportunities for nurturing latent Islamic sentiments in Uzbekistan and Tajikistan, but these are not good.

RELATIONS WITH PAKISTAN AND INDIA

In recent years, Iran and Pakistan have often found common ground arising from geography, mutual opposition to Soviet influence, their Islamic constitutions and troubled relations with the United States. Leaders in both states have called for stronger ties and enhanced cooperation on regional issues. Both countries are founding members of the Economic Cooperation Organization that now includes Central Asian countries. Both have been deeply affected by the protracted conflict in Afghanistan with refugees and militants creating havoc in their border areas. Though Iran and Pakistan see themselves as mediators, their different approaches and allies in Afghanistan have occasionally caused friction. Rumors of a possible military alliance, including nuclear weapons cooperation, between the two have surfaced; India is clearly apprehensive about this possibility.[18]

Good relations with India could be of great benefit to Iran both from a geopolitical and economic perspective. India, however, remains ambivalent about Iran. On the one hand, the most recent annual report to Parliament by the Indian Defense Ministry noted that "Iran stands out conspicuously in terms of rapid military buildup and modernization of its forces with particular emphasis on missile arsenal, air force and force projection capabilities."[19] It was the first time that the defense ministry report included a reference to any state but Pakistan and China. India is worried primarily not about Iran's buildup per se, but about the strategic linkages between Iran and Pakistan. Expanded linkages may mean military cooperation between the latter two states as well as an increased degree of influence from Islamic Iranian and Pakistani visionaries over India's Muslims.

On the other hand, Prime Minister P.V. Narasimha Rao's visit to Iran in September 1993 served as a platform for cooperative Indo-Iranian rhetoric. Both Rao and Rafsanjani spoke of building stronger economic ties and studying ways of enhancing peace and security in the region. According to the *Times of India*, the "two leaders held wide-ranging discussions on international, regional and bilateral issues of mutual concern."[20] During Rao's visit Iran allegedly reiterated that it considers Kashmir an internal Indian matter, and it publicly denounced terrorism as a means of settling contentious issues—a clear reference to Pakistani intervention in Kashmir. Indian editorials lauded the visit, describing it as a watershed in Indo-Iranian relations.[21]

IRAN AND THE GULF ARABS

Iran's relations with the Gulf Arab countries operate on two tracks: on the one hand is a decided need to cultivate friends and escape regional isolation; on the other hand, Iran nurtures a desire to assert an independent and forceful foreign policy. It is open to question whether Iran's leaders have the skill and acumen needed to balance these two often contradictory goals. Indeed, relations between Iran and its Arab neighbors have been strained for decades, especially since the revolution. Fearful of Islamic revivalism, most Arab states supported Iraq during the Iran-Iraq War.

The 1991 Gulf War marked a turning point in Iran's relations with its Gulf neighbors. Taking advantage of Iraq's pariah status, Iran opposed the invasion and took steps toward improving ties with Saudi Arabia and the other Gulf countries. Even during this period of conciliation, one contentious issue divided Iran and the GCC states: Iran's staunch opposition to the Western military presence in the Persian Gulf. Whereas the Gulf states welcomed the United States, Iran feared an enhanced American military role in the region. In the war's aftermath, Iran believes the GCC states have deliberately excluded it from regional security arrangements. Iran points to the Damascus Declaration, an agreement issued by the GCC with Egypt and Syria in March 1991, which set up on paper an Arab peace force without Iran.

Though they abandoned the notion of collective security and never ratified the Damascus Declaration, the pragmatic Gulf sheikhdoms began searching for other ways to counter their bigger neighbors, Iran and Iraq. Specifically, the Gulf states have grown increasingly apprehensive that Iran is determined to become the regional hegemon. Moreover, Iran's conciliatory moves have been obscured by its bullying tactics on the island of Abu Musa and its military buildup. (A fuller explanation of the

Abu Musa controversy is provided in the following endnote.[22])

Since the Iraqi invasion of Kuwait in August 1990, Kuwait, Bahrain, Qatar and Oman have all signed defense cooperation agreements with the United States; the United Arab Emirates (UAE) is close to an agreement. A less formalized arrangement with Saudi Arabia is also in place. The Saudis are buying sophisticated American weapons and participating in joint military exercises. In addition, the GCC states are expanding their economic ties with the West by bringing in French, Italian, American and Japanese partners for oil development projects.[23]

There is no truce in sight for the Gulf Arabs and Iran. The bickering that followed the GCC's Abu Dhabi Declaration in December 1992 demonstrated that relations are tenuous at best.[24] After the GCC reaffirmed its rejection of Iran's occupation of Abu Musa, Iran's Foreign Ministry issued a blistering statement labeling the GCC statement "worthless" and indicating that it represented an "irresponsible stand."[25] At a 1993 meeting in Riyadh, the Gulf ministers reaffirmed their support for the United Arab Emirates and claimed that Iran's actions continue to threaten regional stability.[26] The UAE plans to take the dispute to the United Nations despite Iran's invitation to resume negotiations over the Gulf islands. Negotiations held in September 1992 collapsed after Teheran refused to discuss two other disputed islands, the Greater and Lesser Tunbs. The Shah of Iran seized the two islands in 1971, but they are still claimed by the UAE.

RELATIONS WITH SPECIFIC GULF COUNTRIES[27]

It is, nevertheless, useful to briefly review the key issues between Iran and each of the Gulf states to show how Iran's presence across the Gulf cannot be ignored and how, in different ways, each has to find its own equilibrium with its powerful neighbor.

Saudi Arabia: Saudi Arabia is the largest, richest and most powerful of the Arab Gulf states. Its close relations with the United States reached a climax during the Gulf War. Without access to Saudi bases the operation to evict Iraq from Kuwait could not have been undertaken. Hence, the status of Saudi-U.S. relations are of critical importance to Iran, fearful as it is of the American military presence in the region. Iranian relations with Saudi Arabia have often been tumultuous. The Hajj, Muslims' annual pilgrimage to Mecca, has been a significant source of conflict. Iran and Saudi Arabia broke off diplomatic relations in 1988 in a dispute over the bloody 1987 Hajj in which 402 pilgrims, including 275 Iranians, died in riots.[28] On March 26, 1991, diplomatic relations were restored. After the Iranian embassy in Saudi Arabia reopened on April 1, 1991, the Saudi government allowed 110,000 Iranian pilgrims, plus 5,000 relatives of those who died in the 1987 incident, to travel to Mecca. More recently, the two nations reached an agreement permitting 115,000 Iranians to participate in the 1993 pilgrimage.[29]

Though controversies surrounding the Hajj may have subsided, Iran and Saudi Arabia are at odds over another issue: the two countries are engaged in a pitched battle to control the OPEC oil cartel. Iran has adopted a familiar Saudi tactic: pushing up oil production before OPEC meetings as a bargaining chip. Commenting on the Iranian maneuver, the *Middle East Economic Survey* warned that "Iran is serving notice to OPEC...that from now on it must be regarded as a member of the excess capacity club, which could add a new dimension to the OPEC bargaining table."[30]

Kuwait: Since Kuwait owes its very existence to the United States, it might be assumed that relations with Iran would be very cool given the animosity between Teheran and Washington. Furthermore, since Kuwait was one of the chief financial supporters of Iraq during the Iran-Iraq War, relations between Kuwait and Iran were bad during that period. Iran's opposition to Iraq's invasion of Kuwait, however, set the stage for a rapprochement between the two countries. As evidence of his commitment to improve relations after the war, President Rafsanjani dispatched $40 million worth of fire-fighting equipment to Kuwait, and a National Iranian Oil Company team began fire-fighting missions on August 5, 1991.[31] In November 1992, Kuwait and Iran signed an agreement on marine transportation. President Rafsanjani met with Kuwait's deputy prime minister and foreign minister in February 1993 and discussed cooperation in OPEC. Nevertheless, Iran's postwar relations with Kuwait have been marred by the issues that affect the GCC as a whole, such as Iran's military buildup and the Abu Musa dispute. The Kuwaiti government takes the issue of Abu Musa seriously, given that its own political legitimacy was threatened by an aggressive alteration of its borders.

United Arab Emirates: Like the other, smaller Gulf states, the UAE has been more receptive to Iranian overtures because of the desire to counter Saudi dominance in the GCC. Although Iran's relationship with the UAE is now dominated by the Abu Musa controversy, relations between the two have traditionally been strong. They have successfully withstood the Iranian revolution and the Iran-Iraq War, and trade ties have flourished. Dubai (one of the emirates) is Iran's largest trading partner in the Gulf.[32] Interestingly enough, Sharjah, the emirate that is embroiled in the Abu Musa controversy, signed an agreement in November 1992 for the joint development of an oil field it shares with Iran located near the disputed island.[33]

Despite the commercial ties, the conflict over Abu Musa guarantees that bilateral relations will be unstable. In February 1993, the UAE President, Shaykh Zayid bin-Sultan al-Nuhayyan, vowed to regain control of the three disputed Gulf islands. Moreover, he stated that the "development of friendly ties between the two countries hinges on boosting confidence and measures that show Iran's adherence to international law and respect of the UAE sovereignty."[34]

Bahrain: Relations with Bahrain have been sensitive because of Iran's now-renounced historical claim to the island state and because of a 1981 coup attempt supposed to have been sponsored by Iran. Nevertheless, relations began improving after the Gulf War. Diplomatic ties were upgraded and commercial links strengthened; shipping lines, direct flights, joint transportation companies and projects for industrial cooperation were established.[35] The Abu Musa conflict has disrupted relations, as Bahrain supports the policy of the GCC toward Iran. In February 1993, the Iranian ambassador to Bahrain, Javad Tork-Abadi, and Bahrain's prime minister, Khalifa bin Salman al-Khalifa, held talks in which they stressed continued development of ties in various fields of mutual interest.[36]

Qatar: Teheran's relations with Qatar are improving. In May 1992, Iranian First Vice-President Hasan Habibi visited Qatar—an event which Iranians regarded as a watershed in relations between the two countries. Later in the same month Qatar's interior minister, Sheikh Abdallah bin Khalifa al-Thani, paid a visit to Iran. As a result of these meetings, Iran and Qatar concluded cooperation agreements covering sea and air transport, the media, agriculture, customs, fisheries, drug trafficking, status of nationals and delivery of fresh water by Iran to Qatar via pipeline.[37] Qatar sees Iran as a counterweight to Saudi dominance. During the Saudi-Qatari border dispute last year, Qatar reportedly turned to Iran for protection against Saudi threats.[38] Qatari-Iranian differences over the North Field natural gas project are discussed elsewhere in this report.

Oman: As the only Persian Gulf state straddling the Gulf of Hormuz across from Iran's shores, Oman shares a mutual strategic interest with Iran. These deep-rooted ties have given Oman incentive to play an active role in mediating between the Arab world and Iran. During the Abu Musa confrontation, Oman has assumed a leading role in negotiating differences between the two sides. More important, in an interview on January 24, 1993, Oman's minister of state for foreign affairs, Yusuf bin Alawi bin Abdallah, reiterated his country's position that the Abu Musa conflict will not result in estrangement between Iran and Oman.[39] In addition, Oman's government at times has attempted to dispel the impression that Iran is bent on regional hegemony. When asked in the same interview about Iran's regional ambitions, arms buildup and support for Islamic fundamentalism, the Omani minister pointed out that all states have ambitions and dismissed the alleged threats as political propaganda.[40]

HOW DANGEROUS IS IRAN?

Iran poses a number of threats to Western interests. These include direct military challenges to the security of the GCC states, possible nuclear, chemical and biological weapons programs, subversion of friendly regimes such as Egypt, acts of terrorism against the regime's opponents and secularists in other Muslim countries and opposition to the Middle East peace process. Given the failure of the Bush administration and the key regional Arab powers to understand Saddam Hussein's intentions in 1990, it is inevitable that the Clinton administration will seek to avoid a similar mistake vis-à-vis Iran. But will this tendency lend itself to exaggerations of Iranian threats? Could such a portrayal of Iran in parts of the U.S. media, Congress and the executive branch strengthen the very groups in Iran that are most antagonistic to America? To arrive at an answer, it is useful to distinguish between overt military threats, on the one hand, and those that relate more to subversion and terrorism, on the other. Iran's human rights abuses, while extreme, do not directly threaten U.S. interests, though they provide much ammunition for Iran's detractors in the West and elsewhere.

MILITARY THREATS

Iran's leaders now believe that superior military power is decisive in shaping the strategic environment in the Middle East. Force, far from being passé, is an essential instrument of power. They learned this lesson the hard way—through their defeat in the Iran-Iraq War and the vivid images of Desert Storm, in which superior American technology and organization vanquished Saddam's highly touted military machine. As a consequence they believe that military preparedness must be granted a high priority by the regime. Iran cannot rely on a "people's war" fought with inferior equipment for its defense—a belief its leaders trumpeted in the early idealistic days of the Iran-Iraq War. Instead, Iran needs large stockpiles of modern weapons and a professional force-in-being. What progress has Iran made, and what sorts of military threats can it now direct against its neighbors and the U.S. military presence? Iran's weapons modernization programs are reviewed in the next sections, followed by a more specific threat analysis.

THE CONVENTIONAL REARMAMENT PROGRAM

Iran is trying to rebuild, restructure and modernize its armed forces. Although it currently has money to buy advanced arms on the international market, and most weapons are not difficult to find, the problem of supplier reliability remains. Russia, for example, may have an ample supply of

arms, but it has yet to demonstrate an ability to provide long-term support to its customers. Service is believed to be unreliable and erratic, and
spare parts are often unavailable.

The lessons of international sanctions imposed on Iran during the
Iran-Iraq War suggest that self-reliance must be one of Iran's long-term
goals if only to avoid future humiliations. This would entail increased domestic production of arms and support items and a decrease in its dependency on foreign supplies. However, the undeveloped state of Iran's domestic armaments industry ensures that weapons produced locally will be
inferior to those purchased on the international arms market. In a new
study by Shahram Chubin produced for the Carnegie Endowment's Middle East Arms Control project, Chubin notes that the self-reliance
scheme has limited feasibility.[1]

To mitigate the impact of continuing U.S. and West European sanctions on arms sales, Iran has developed supply relationships with Russia
and some of the remaining communist states to buy new aircraft, submarines, tanks and missiles. While their service leaves much to be desired, Russia, North Korea and China manage to provide some advanced
conventional weaponry. The reduction of East-West tensions in Europe
has given rise to surplus weaponry and a buyers' market. Iran's modernization program should benefit from the arms glut; the problem remains,
however, that while arms supplies from multiple sources may tend to reduce the hardships of future sanctions, the inefficiencies of operating different weapons from different suppliers tend to increase.

While the Central Intelligence Agency estimates that Iran is spending
$2 billion on arms purchases, fluctuating exchange rates, barter deals and
domestic production give this and any such figure a large margin of
error.[2] The Iranian minister of defense, Akbar Torkan, claims that Iran's
entire defense budget in 1993 is only $850 million.[3] A better indicator
than the actual numbers, however, is the general trend of an across-the-
board buildup. Chubin notes that Iran is rebuilding its military forces,
modernizing its equipment and seeking the most advanced arms where
possible. These developments do not necessarily imply aggressive intent.
In his view, this is still a reasonable program given Iranian needs and
comparisons with past Iranian force levels and those of neighboring
states; Iran still has a long way to go to be militarily effective. Chubin's
conclusions on this point are similar to those of three well informed
American defense specialists, Anthony Cordesman, W. Seth Carus and
Henry Sokolski.[4]

If these trends continue and anticipated purchases materialize, Iran could eventually develop a much enhanced sea-denial capability. Its acquisition plans include Russian Kilo-class diesel submarines, Russian SU-24 Fencer attack aircraft, Chinese Silkworm antiship missiles and, possibly, the Russian TU-22M Backfire bomber armed with the Kitchen stand-off air-to-surface missile. Chubin argues that if Iran continues its naval buildup, especially by developing its missile and amphibious capabilities, its neighbors will grow increasingly suspicious of it real intentions. Certain additions would allow the Iranian navy to disrupt shipping. With a coastline far longer than Iraq's and more widely dispersed naval assets, Chubin suggests that Iran could slow the access of major ships through the Persian Gulf and cause trouble for U.S. forces. In Chubin's opinion, potential Iranian anti-naval capabilities are the greatest source of concern in the conventional weapons arena.

All evaluations of Iran's capabilities are dogged by the paucity of concrete facts about the Iranian buying spree, however. This creates uneasiness as to the accuracy of available estimates. A modernization program is underway, but there is no sense of its parameters. Observers have difficulty assessing the buildup, especially without an end point in sight. Moreover, Iran has yet to decide on an appropriate force structure and doctrine, assure continuity of arms suppliers, standardize its hybrid equipment, replenish stocks and upgrade existing equipment. These are not easy tasks.

There are, of course, more benign explanations as to what is happening. A comparison of the current inventory against Iran's forces at the peak of the Shah's buildup in 1978-79 reveals that Iran has only one-third to one-half of former arms levels. It has less than half as many tanks as at the time of the Shah's fall, and most of these are outdated and improperly equipped for night warfare. Iran has a good amount of tube artillery, but is unable to use it properly since it lacks the fire control and target systems. Iran's approximately one hundred attack helicopters date back to the 1970s. Compared with its well-armed neighbors, Iraq and Saudi Arabia, Iran's potential military threat diminishes. And unlike Iraq and Saudi Arabia, Iran has not been a profligate spender on arms. In fact, if one accepts the 1979 baseline year, trends in military capability and balance have shifted against Iran. Relying on such benchmarks, Chubin concludes that the buildup at this stage is less threatening than many have suggested.

UNCERTAINTIES ABOUT THE BUILDUP

To illustrate the problems of analyzing the conventional buildup it is worth reviewing what has been reported, and, more importantly, what is known about the status of four very significant weapons: SU-24 aircraft, TU-22M bombers, surface-to-surface missiles and Kilo-class submarines. If Iran received these weapons in large numbers and had the capabilities to operate and maintain them, this would indeed represent a major and dangerous shift in the regional balance.

Two military combat aircraft are particularly relevant in the context of Gulf security and American contingency planning for the region, the Russian-made SU-24 Fencer and the TU-22M Backfire bomber. The Fencer is a long-range strike and interdiction aircraft equivalent to the U.S. F-111. It provides Iran with deep-strike capabilities and would extend the reach of the Iranian air force to targets well inside Saudi territory if used in a cross-Gulf war. Its weapons include air-to-air missiles, air-to-surface missiles, cannons and, in its configuration for use in the Soviet air force, nuclear weapons. The maximum weapons load is 8,000 kilograms (17,600 pounds) and the combat radius for standard warload in normal configuration is 320 kilometers (192 miles) if the plane is flying in the so-called lo-lo-lo profile and 1,130 kilometers (678 miles) for a high-lo-high profile.[6] In short, this is a formidable capability. According to the International Institute for Strategic Studies (IISS), as of fall 1993, ten aircraft had been delivered to supplement ten already in Iran. The IISS also reported that twenty-five additional aircraft had been ordered, though other reports suggest that Iran has backed out of an ongoing deal with the Russians to purchase an additional two squadrons (approximately forty aircraft) because of uncertainty over spare parts and logistical backup.[7]

Although Iran may have deployed the SU-24 in small numbers, professional analysts estimate that it will take three to five years for these planes to be fully integrated into its inventory. The main problems concern pilot training and access to spare parts.[8]

The TU-22M Backfire bomber, built for a Soviet confrontation with the United States, posed a major threat to the U.S. Navy when operating in the Arctic Ocean, the Mediterranean and the Far East. The Backfire is a bomber and a maritime reconnaissance/attack aircraft. It has a 4,000-kilometer (2,400-mile) unrefueled combat radius. If introduced into the Iranian inventory, it would be the only strategic bomber in the region with an unrefueled combat radius covering the entire Middle East. In its Soviet role, it was capable of performing nuclear strikes, conventional attacks and antiship missions. It has a maximum weapons load of 12,000 kilograms (26,400 pounds) and can carry air-to-surface missiles or 12,000 kilograms of conventional ordinance. It is capable of carrying three 180-kilometer (108-mile) range Kitchen antiship missiles which have warheads configured to cripple or sink U.S. aircraft carriers at attack speeds of Mach 3. According to Sokolski, if several Backfires with Kitchens attack a U.S. carrier group in a coordinated mode, they are virtually impossible to defeat.[9]

Despite the formidable capability of the TU-22M bomber, whether Iran will acquire it soon or at all remains uncertain. There are unconfirmed reports of an arms deal with Russia in mid-1992.[10] Some of the reports say that the deal was worth $2 billion.[11] One report in August 1992 speculated that Iran might have already acquired the TU-22M.[12] Yet reports from March 1993 suggest that Iran has canceled much of the alleged deal, though it still wants this component of the package.[13] Chubin believes that Iranian acquisition of the TU-22M is highly unlikely.

As far as surface-to-surface missiles are concerned, the Iranians may be procuring SCUD-Bs and -Cs from North Korea. The SCUD-B has a 300-kilometer (180-mile) range with a payload of 1,000 kilograms (2,200 pounds). The SCUD-C has a 500-kilometer (300-mile) range with a payload of 700 kilograms (1,540 pounds).[14] In 1992, North Korean ships were reported to have delivered SCUDs to Iranian ports, though both Iranian and North Korean officials denied this. Another 1992 report stated that Iran had purchased 170 SCUDs though it was not clear as to which variety.[15] Most relevant, the Nodong is a new missile developed by North Korea with a range of 1,000 kilometers (600 miles). There are reports that the Nodong has been purchased by Iran and that it will be delivered in the coming months. One report suggests that Iran has ordered 150, but there is no evidence yet of any Nodongs in service.[16] If the Nodong does indeed have a range of 1,000 kilometers, it would, in theory, be able to reach Israel from bases in Western Iran. In addition to North Korean missiles, Western officials believe that Libya has sold the design of its Al-Fatah medium-range missile to Iran. This missile is believed to have a range of up to 950 kilometers (570 miles) and a payload of 500 kilograms (1,100 pounds).[17]

The Kilo-class submarine is a diesel electric submarine. Its main armament is eighteen type-53 533-millimeter dual-purpose torpedoes. The torpedoes have the capacity to lay up to twenty-four mines, each with 1,000 pounds (455 kilograms) of explosives.[18] The submarines are also probably equipped to launch surface-to-air missiles such as the SA-14 Gremlin or SA-16 Gimlet.[19] The great advantage of the Kilo-class submarines is that they are hard to detect with acoustic devices. They do have to resurface in order to recharge, but they can sit for long periods on the sea bed and cannot be heard. According to reports, the submarines will be based at Chah Bahar along the Gulf of Oman. The first submarine, named Tariq, was formally inducted into the Iranian navy at Bandar Abbas on November 23, 1992.[20] It is understood that the second submarine has been delivered and that Iran has an option to take delivery of a third. In addition to the submarines, Iran has a large stock of modern mines which can be laid by submarines, surface vessels and aircraft.

This brief review suggests that the record is very blurry as far as the transfer of these key weapons are concerned. For the next year or so, Iran will pose no real sea-denial threat to the United States. Serious threats could emerge in the mid-1990s *if* the buildup continues, *if* Iran is capable of servicing and maintaining the weapons and *if* it can conduct the requisite training of personnel. There are doubts on the part of many observers that Iran will be able to do any of this, although in view of past misjudgments about developing countries' capabilities, it would be foolish to bank on such inefficiency.

OTHER COMPLICATING FACTORS

It is difficult to determine Iranian military strategy from its procurement policy. Iran has a tendency to overstock weapons while the suppliers' window is open since no supplier values its relationship with Iran over one with the United States. Growing American pressure (including new laws) to restrain foreign sales to Iran threatens to cut off supplies at any time. Despite the oft-presumed linkage between procurement policy and force structure, Iran does not necessarily buy certain equipment to develop particular capabilities. As Chubin notes, regardless of the possibility of new arms, nothing as yet suggests that Iran will be more prone to using force in the future.

Iran's military suffers from poor systems integration because of its procurement weaknesses. For example, it has some fifty to sixty Soviet SA-2 and the Chinese HQ-2J surface-to-surface missiles, but they are not compatible. The software needed to integrate them is not available to Iran. Its military is far from having an integrated air defense system. Combined with the split between the much-maligned professional army and the Revolutionary Guard, the overall state of preparedness of the military is low, and quality equipment is often wasted.[21]

Iran's modernization program is likely to suffer from the effects of switching suppliers. As Iran moves from Western to Soviet-designed equipment, numerous problems will arise in training, maintenance, doctrine and the availability of spare parts. There is a long history of attempts by developing countries to change their major suppliers and the difficulties they encounter. In a related situation, Egypt experienced problems as their forces moved from East bloc weapons to mainly American systems. According to Chubin, the Iranian changeover might require an adjustment period of a decade or longer. Such a severe restraint on the Iranian buildup significantly undermines Iran's short-term ability to live up to its hegemonic reputation.

Assessing the capabilities of the Revolutionary Guard in the conventional equation is difficult. It often gets the best equipment, preventing its integration into the regular armed forces. But its ideological drive has failed to translate into impressive military prowess. It clearly has the potential to play a key role in a wide range of issues as the regime's designated representative of revolutionary ideals.[22] Chubin explains that the Iranian leadership's ideal armed forces would have the professionalism and skills of the regular army and the commitment to the revolution of the Revolutionary Guard. No apparent means of achieving this is forthcoming. The current mismatch of zealous but ill-trained troops and sophisticated systems limits the effectiveness of advanced arms.

IRAN'S WEAPONS OF MASS DESTRUCTION

There is widespread belief in Western intelligence circles that Iran has embarked on a covert nuclear weapons program. If true, it would represent a new, dangerous threat to the Middle East and would eclipse all other points of contention. The possibility arouses particularly keen anxiety because of the Iraqi experience, in which the intelligence community consistently underestimated the Iraqi nuclear program. Since that time, there is added concern as well over the security of nuclear weapons and their associated technologies in the former Soviet Union. The specter of an oil-rich Middle East country which harbors nuclear ambitions finding it much easier to circumvent control regimes in pursuit of covert nuclear options is very well substantiated.

There are undoubtedly individuals within the Islamic Republic's hierarchy who see a utility in Iran's pursuing a nuclear weapons program and may indeed have advocated such an option to Rafsanjani. Chubin writes that Iran is a serious candidate for nuclear weapons acquisition. He argues that the experience and lessons of the past fifteen years and the current hostile regional and international environment led Iran to conclude that chemical and nuclear weapons are necessary and prudent hedges for its future defense. There is strong evidence that the Iranians are engaged in a modest nuclear research program with possible military implications. To this extent, Iran's purchase of nuclear research reactors from China has greater implications for weapons development than does the proposed purchase of nuclear power reactors from Russia because Russia has insisted that Iran abide by international supervision and nonproliferation norms.[23]

However, confusion abounds regarding the evidence that the Iranians are physically assembling the infrastructure and the teams necessary for a full-fledged nuclear weapons program similar to those developed by Israel, India, Iraq, North Korea and Pakistan. In 1992 Iran permitted the International Atomic Energy Agency (IAEA) to inspect its listed nuclear facilities and other installations alleged to contain nuclear activity. On this occasion, the IAEA found no incriminating evidence of illegal actions when it returned from the mission, though some doubt exists within the intelligence community as to whether the IAEA team looked in the right places. Based on what has been published in the open literature, there is no known secret facility in Iran that is physically engaged in the process of building components for nuclear weapons at this time.

Iran's nuclear activity poses so potentially serious a threat because of the availability of hard currency generated from oil sales over the past year. While Iran has huge domestic needs, its hard currency revenues are sufficiently large in aggregate terms that if a small percentage were siphoned off to support nuclear activity, it would amount to a sizable sum. It might be enough to tempt countries or individuals hard-pressed for money to sell Iran the necessary knowledge or technology. Furthermore, Iran has a population of close to 60 million and a significant number of well-educated scientists and engineers. Economic crisis is not necessarily a hindrance in this arena. Pakistan and India, though ranked among the poorest countries in the world, were able to develop first-rate nuclear cadres. The experiences of the Soviet Union, China and North Korea—poor countries in macroeconomic terms—further illustrate how advanced national security projects can be developed if major resources are allocated to such ends on a priority basis.

Concern about the Iranian program is compounded by stories in the press alleging the purchase of nuclear weapons by Iran from such countries as Kazakhstan. Some argue that these stories are part of a deliberate deception plan launched by the Mojahedin opposition and Israel, both of whom wish to draw attention to Iran's nuclear intentions. There is evidence that several international swindling operations have been attempted. Apparently, groups of people from the former Soviet Union claim to have access to nuclear materials and try to peddle their "products" to countries such as Iran for large sums paid up front. Kazakhstan allegedly promised Israeli officials that it would not assist an Iranian nuclear weapons program.[24]

The uncertainty about the nuclear program poses a policy dilemma for the United States. Elevating concerns about an Iranian bomb to the top of the list of priorities may weaken U.S. credibility on a whole array of technology-transfer issues and undermine nonproliferation strategies elsewhere. Furthermore, strident American rhetoric that includes discussion of preemptive or covert operations against Iran to stop its nuclear weapons program could have precisely the reverse effect. It could strengthen the position of those in Iran who believe the United States is a threat to the existence of the republic; they might consequently prevail in an argument over whether or not to launch a crash effort to produce a nuclear weapon.

On the other hand, taking a relaxed approach and dismissing nuclear rumblings as Mojahedin and Zionist propaganda is more irresponsible. It is essential to focus intelligence efforts on Iran to make sure that nuclear programs are not proceeding. If they are, the West must heighten controls on exports, enact sanctions against those countries or individuals who are party to proliferation and compel the IAEA to conduct more spot inspections of suspicious Iranian facilities.

Some analysts argue that dangers will remain even if there are foolproof assurances that Iran is not obtaining black market nuclear items from the former Soviet Union, North Korea, China or Pakistan, and it continues to adhere to NPT (Nuclear Non-Proliferation Treaty) and IAEA rules of inspection. What Iran can legitimately do under such safeguards is to develop the infrastructure and specialist training in nuclear engineering that could at some point in the future be turned to weapons use if Iran was prepared to withdraw from the NPT or embark on a covert program as both Iraq and North Korea have done. The only way to prevent such a contingency would be to deny Iran *all* opportunities to develop a nuclear infrastructure. It is highly unlikely this could ever be done except as part of a complete denuclearization of the Middle East.[25]

In turn, Iran's nuclear ambitions are bound to be influenced by how credible the international community is in persuading Iran that Iraqi nuclear weapons are under permanent international control. Iran must be convinced that an Iraqi program will not reemerge once new leadership comes to power in Baghdad. This will not be an easy task since Iraq, even more than Iran, may be able to restart its weapons programs covertly once its huge oil revenues are restored.[26] A tough U.S. nonproliferation policy must heighten the intelligence activities, confirm or deny all rumors, assure that no leakage occurs from the former Soviet Union, prevent nuclear deals with China, Pakistan or North Korea and monitor carefully all developments in the high-tech field that suggest, based on the experience with Iraq, that a weapons program might be in the offing. However, in the long run it is important to include Iran in any arms control regime in the Middle East. Such a move is necessary if only to bring the Israelis on board; Israel will never agree to Middle East arms control regimes involving nuclear weapons unless Iran, and probably Pakistan, are subject to strict verification standards.

In addition to a possible nuclear weapons program, some analysts, most notably Anthony Cordesman, express concern about Iran's nascent biological weapons programs. Cordesman argues that there is strong evidence Iran is developing these weapons and is making efforts to obtain the appropriate technology from Switzerland and Germany. Once developed, biological agents could, in theory, be used for both terrorist and regular military operations.[27] Iran also has the capability to produce chemical weapons, though there is some controversy as to whether it can presently produce nerve gas.[28]

ANALYSIS OF THE MILITARY THREATS

While much of the discussion on Iran's buildup remains speculative, the United States and its Gulf allies know for certain that an increase in Iran's military capabilities will require significant changes in contingency plans. One way to assess what this means is to compare the military threats posed by Iraq in 1990 to those Iran could pose in several years to the Arab Gulf and its oil resources.

The Iraqi threat emanated from its formidable land and air forces. These forces were able to overrun Kuwait in August 1990 and could have moved onward into Saudi Arabia and its major oil fields without encountering serious ground opposition. The tiny Iraqi navy played a negligible role in the invasion and contributed little to the campaign during Desert Storm. Had Saddam Hussein chosen a more conservative strategy and limited his invasion to an incursion into northern Kuwait, or, alternatively, had he not stopped at the Saudi border and proceeded to capture the oil fields, the crisis might have turned out quite differently.

It is unlikely that any military confrontation with Iran would be a replay of Desert Storm. While there has been steady progress in military cooperation between the U.S. and the GCC, other factors suggest a more complex, less reassuring scenario. The coincidence of timing, luck and circumstance that befell Desert Storm was extraordinary. A unique alliance embracing the U.N. Security Council, the key Arab countries, Turkey, the Soviet Union and Western Europe provided the United States with the political authority to mount the most massive and well prepared military operation since World War Two. With access to superb land bases in Saudi Arabia and secure lines of communication; six months to complete the military preparations; an army, navy and air force at peak efficiency and morale; and an opponent outgunned by technology and led by a stupid leader, it is not surprising that the war was won so easily.

Iran currently poses no significant land threat to any of its Gulf neighbors, including Iraq. Iran's army and air forces would face more severe logistical problems in projecting power into the Arab Gulf states than Iraq encountered. A land invasion of the Arabian peninsula would require initial confrontation with Iraq which still has the largest ground forces in the region. Any attack across the Gulf waters would require major amphibious and air lift capabilities which are presently beyond Iran's capabilities.

Nevertheless, Iran is a maritime power with 2,440 kilometers (1,464 miles) of coastline (excluding the Caspian Sea) and a much stronger naval tradition than Iraq. Beyond simple acts of intimidation against its weaker neighbors, Iran could pose dangers for U.S. and GCC maritime operations if its sea-denial capabilities continue to improve. U.S. aircraft carriers would probably not risk entering the Gulf in the event of likely hostilities with Iran, at least in the early days of confrontation. Hence they would be limited to air operations from positions in the Arabian Sea and the Gulf of Oman. This, in turn, would limit the range and intensity of naval air operations over Iranian targets, especially those north of Isfahan. The most serious naval challenge to the American fleet would be posed by a combination of submarines, mines, surface-to-surface missiles and long-range strike aircraft with stand-off missiles. While U.S. carriers based outside the Gulf could conduct isolated bombing raids deep into Iran, this could not be done on a sustained basis without land-based air-refueling facilities. Even so, the U.S. Navy could not conduct the type of air operations that the U.S. air forces, including the navy, conducted during Desert Storm when the Gulf itself was a benign environment and extensive use of Saudi air bases was possible.

Iran could also pose a threat to sea traffic in the Gulf, including the Strait of Hormuz. This could be self-defeating however. Any effort by the Iranians to close the Gulf would shut off their own oil exports, which are vital for their survival. They have no alternative land routes at this time that could make up for the loss of the sea routes. An Iranian effort to mine the Strait of Hormuz would be likely to prove extremely difficult given the depths of the strait and its powerful currents. By far Iran's most effective use of mines against the United States would be as a terror tactic—to hit a U.S. ship and cause great loss of life—rather than to seriously interfere with military operations.

If Iran possessed nuclear weapons it would change the entire nature of the confrontation, and the United States would be faced with the dilemma that might have arisen vis-à-vis Iraq had Saddam Hussein had nuclear weapons. The U.S. military establishment must therefore carefully monitor the Iranian buildup, and be prepared to adjust the contingency plans, particularly if the nuclear weapons program continues to expand and sea-denial capabilities grow.[29]

To conclude, there is little likelihood that Iran can pose much of a conventional threat to the Gulf so long as the United States maintains a strong forward military presence, expands defense cooperation with the GCC countries, continues to be effective in limiting technology and Western arms supplies to Iran, maintains cooperative relations with Russia and can command wide ranging political support throughout the Middle East. If however some of these conditions were to change — a greater than anticipated cutback in the U.S. defense budget, a change of regime in Saudi Arabia or Egypt, a more assertive Russia — it is not hard to think of scenarios when Iran's military challenges would be more difficult to counter. The United States cannot assume that the next major crisis in the Gulf will be a repeat of Desert Shield and Desert Storm.

TERRORISM AND SUBVERSION

While Iran's military potential poses a long-term threat to the United States, there are other causes for more immediate concern. They are Iran's subversion of friendly regimes, its support for terrorism and its rejection of the Arab-Israeli peace process. If Iran and its rejectionist allies succeed in promoting radical regimes in the Middle East, American military power, no matter how great, may not be sufficient to prevent the erosion of stability and increasing threat to the Gulf itself.

Iran's Activities in Sudan and North Africa

On August 18, 1993, the U.S. government announced that Sudan would be added to the State Department's list of countries supporting terrorism based on evidence that Sudan harbors such terrorist groups as Hizbollah and the Palestinian Islamic Jihad. The action underlined Sudan's ever-growing link to Iran, which is a main supporter of these organizations.

Since the coup d'etat of 1989 which overthrew the democratically elected Sudanese government of Sadiq el-Mahdi, Iran has fashioned a public alliance with Sudan's Muslim fundamentalist regime. Teheran supplies Sudan with arms and ammunition and uses it as a training ground for Islamic and Palestinian terrorists.

Indications of the growing links between Teheran and Khartoum include Rafsanjani's visit to Sudan in December 1991, reciprocated by a high-level Sudanese military delegation's voyage to Iran in the summer of 1992. The delegation sought augmented backing for the government's war against rebels in southern Sudan. Furthermore, the Revolutionary Guard trains Sudan's national militia, which functions as an adjunct to the armed forces.[30]

The extent of Iranian influence over Sudan remains unclear. Sudan, after all, is a Sunni state, and it has been dependent on substantial amounts of aid from such fellow Sunni states as Saudi Arabia. Shiite-Sunni relations, on the other hand, have traditionally been poor. But some observers fear that Sudan has become Iran's "new satellite" and that Teheran's infiltration runs deep, including the establishment of military training camps and intelligence outposts.[31]

In addition to U.S. government concerns, officials in Tunisia, Saudi Arabia, Egypt and Algeria contend that Sudan is a launching pad for Iranian-style militancy and the supplier of significant logistical support for terrorist organizations across the region.[32] Egyptian officials and media spokesmen have initiated a large-scale campaign to assign blame to Iran and Sudan for the surge of violence within Egypt. The Egyptian government holds Iran directly responsible for training and supporting Islamic militants. As part of the Islamic Group, these militants are engaged in a full-scale war with President Hosni Mubarak's government. The wave of terrorist attacks has caused more than two hundred deaths over the past couple years, forcing the government to intensify its efforts to seize extremists.[33] The attacks, which are aimed at foreign tourists, Coptic Christians, soldiers, police officers, government officials and intellectuals, have significantly affected the country's tourism revenues.

Egypt sees the incidents as part of a crusade to propagate Iran's interpretation of Islam and government.[34] Mubarak has condemned such warped missionary activities, declaring that Iran "is not the guardian of anyone and has no right to speak in the name of Islam and its teachings."[35] An Interior Ministry source stated that interrogation of terrorists revealed a plan to continue the attacks in a bid to "destabilize the country."[36] *Misr al-Fatah* reported that a terrorist front financed by Iran includes Sudan, Algeria's Islamic Salvation Front, Hamas and Egypt's al-Jihad movement. The front has been organized, according to an "official

security source," to spread terrorism in Egypt.[37] Iran has repeatedly denied any connection to terrorist groups or incidents within Egypt.

Arab officials also allege that Iran is supporting Tunisia's banned al-
Nahda fundamentalist movement and the Islamic Salvation Front in Algeria. Sources at the Iranian Foreign Ministry stated in November 1992
that Teheran is committed to support "the legitimate Algerian revolution
against tyranny and arrogance."[38] Algeria had issued regular condemna-
tions of Iran for supporting Algerian fundamentalists, and eventually Algerian officials decided to break off diplomatic relations. In January 1992,
Algeria recalled its ambassador from Teheran. In November, ties were
reduced to a symbolic level. Finally, on March 27, 1993, Algeria announced that after "analyzing the international situation and particularly
the interference of certain countries in Algeria's internal affairs, as well as
their declared support for terrorism, the High Committee of State has
decided to break diplomatic relations with Iran and recall our ambassador
to Sudan."[39] Algeria has blamed "terrorism" by Islamic militants for six
hundred deaths over the past year.

To many Iranian officials, the willingness of Western and Arab countries
to publicize Iran's complicity appears hypocritical and self-serving. These
countries falsely blame Iran for indigenous opposition movements that har-
bor legitimate grievances. The West intervenes militarily and espouses violence in selected cases but denounces Iran for anything but the most passive
foreign policy. This patent double standard, as they see it, puts Iran on the
defensive and casts it as an all-purpose enemy for domestic audiences.

Terrorism against the Regime's Opponents
In a statement of March 5, 1993, the State Department announced that
"Iran is currently the most dangerous state sponsor of terrorism." The
statement noted Iranian involvement in bombings and assassinations
around the world, and called it "the world's principal sponsor of extremist Islamic and Palestinian groups." A few weeks later, Secretary of State
Warren Christopher, in testimony before the Senate Appropriations
Committee's Subcommittee on Foreign Operations, repeated that Iran is
"one of the principal sources of support for terrorist groups around the
world."[40]

Iran has been directly implicated in assassinations of key enemies of
the regime living in Europe. In December 1993, Iranian scholar Mansour
Farhang claimed that 59 exiled Iranian dissidents have been assassinated
since 1979.[41] The Shah's nephew, Prince Shahriyar Shafiq, was killed in
Paris in 1979. General Ghulam Hosein Ovaisi, former commander of the

Iranian land forces under the Shah, was assassinated in Paris in 1984.[42] In August 1991, an Iranian hit squad murdered former Iranian Prime Minister Shapur Bakhtiar near Paris; subsequent French investigations directly linked the murder to the Iranian government.[43]

Iran has also been implicated in attacks on Israeli targets. Iranian operatives have been linked to the March 17, 1992, bombing of the Israeli embassy in Buenos Aires in which nearly thirty people were killed. The Iranian government has repeatedly denied any connection. On May 8, 1992, the U.S. Department of State alleged Iranian involvement in the attack.[44] Other incidents include the March 7, 1992, slaying of Ehud Sadan, chief security officer at the Israeli embassy in Turkey, and the March 1, 1992, hand grenade attack on the Neve Shalom synagogue in Istanbul. The Islamic Jihad and the Islamic Revenge Organization claimed responsibility for the embassy slaying while the synagogue attack was reportedly linked by police to Hizbollah.[45]

Iranian involvement in terrorist attacks in Turkey has also been alleged. Following the January 24, 1993, death of prominent Turkish journalist Ugur Mumcu, segments of the Turkish press accused Iran of orchestrating the fatal car bombing. Mumcu was a strong critic of Islamic fundamentalism, and the Islamic Liberation Army claimed responsibility for the killing. Prime Minister Demirel cautioned against hasty conclusions while admitting that evidence of links to Iran would create "a very delicate situation."[46] In early February, Turkish Interior Minister Ismet Sezgin announced the arrest of nineteen members of a group called Islamic Action that he claimed had been trained in Iran. They were charged with the murder of two prosecular journalists, including Mumcu, and an Iranian dissident, Ali Akbar Ghorbani. Ghorbani had been a member of the People's Mojahedin.[47]

Iran supports several organizations that have well established records of committing acts of terrorism:

Hizbollah: Iran offers financial, political and logistical support for Hizbollah's paramilitary operations in Lebanon. Hizbollah is strongly anti-American and anti-Israel. Although some operations are not approved by Iran, the U.S. Department of State reports that Hizbollah is closely allied with and often directed by Iran. Iranian aid includes training, weapons and explosives. Hizbollah controlled many of the Western hostages in Lebanon and has been a suspect in such major terrorist incidents as the 1983 bombing of U.S. Marine headquarters in Beirut.[48] In late 1992, U.S.

and Arab officials blamed Iran and Hizbollah for attacks on Israeli forces in southern Lebanon.[49]

Hamas: Iran has recently established firm ties with Hamas, which has been active in the Israeli-occupied territories since the start of the Intifada (the uprising). In October 1992, Hamas opened an office in Teheran, and Iran agreed to provide training and funding to Hamas fighters.[50] In April 1993 Hamas was placed on the list of terrorist organizations in the U.S. Department of State's annual report on terrorism. The report cited Iran as one source of its funding.[51]

Popular Liberation Front: Although Syria is its major benefactor, the General Command of the Popular Front for the Liberation of Palestine also receives financial and material support from Iran. The guerrilla militia focuses on cross-border attacks against Israel.[52]

Palestinian Islamic Jihad: The Palestinian Islamic Jihad supports an Islamic Palestinian state and the elimination of Israel. Consequently, it considers the United States an enemy. The U.S. Department of State described the source of their external support as "uncertain, possibly [including] Iran and Syria."[53]

Iran's Rejection of Israel and the Peace Process

The Iranian government severed relations with Israel in February 1979, soon after the overthrow of the Shah. The Islamic Republic has always rejected Israel's right to exist and supported the more rejectionist elements of the Palestinian movement. Its references to Israel are cloaked in anti-Zionist rhetoric: "occupied Palestine," "the illegal Zionist entity" and "Muslim Palestine." One Iranian newspaper claimed that the Jewish Agency, a quasi-governmental Israeli institution, brought in "European Jews to usurp control of Muslim Palestine," adding that Israel "gradually expanded its illegal existence over the past few decades." In a further sign of opposition, Foreign Minister Velayati, in a meeting with Lebanese allies, was reported to have "pledged the Islamic Republic of Iran's full support for Palestine's Islamic uprising and for the expansion of that uprising until the complete overthrow of the Zionist regime."[54] Israel was founded illegally and had no right to continue suppressing the true owners of the land, the Palestinian people.

Since the Madrid peace conference in late 1991 created a new dynamic in the Middle East, Iran has steadfastly opposed the peace negotiations.

Even after the stunning Israel-PLO breakthrough in September 1993, Iran has continued to trumpet this rejectionist line. While the Israeli-Palestinian agreement could have been used by Iran as a cover to change course and support a negotiated settlement, evidence to date suggests no change, simply continued Iranian hostility. This stance could have serious repercussions for relations with key trading partners as Japan and the West European countries where support for the Israel-PLO agreement is strong.

The Madrid process generated new expectations and hopes among governments and individuals in the region. All the direct parties to the conflict committed themselves to a process that seeks a peaceful resolution of the Arab-Israeli conflict. They accepted dialogue as a legitimate vehicle for conflict resolution. Those supporting the peace process demonstrated at least a temporary break with the rejectionist and militant positions of all sides. Iran adamantly opposes the process. When the Madrid talks opened on October 30, 1991, Khamenei called them "a great injustice against the Palestinian nation." Majles deputy Ali Akbar Mohtashemi declared that "participation in this American conference is a treason against Islam and Muslims and the participants are considered as those who have waged war and may be killed with impunity." The Islamic Republic News Agency (IRNA) reported that most Muslims considered the opening as a "day of shame and grief."[55] Nearly one year later, Teheran Radio reiterated the Iranian position in a commentary stating that "it has always been clear and evident that peace talks will bear nothing for Arabs but failure and defeat."[56]

Support for Hizbollah and other terror groups is another manifestation of Iranian opposition to the peace process. Hizbollah, Hamas or other militant groups aligned with Iran can be used to disrupt the process and rattle participants. With a new Hamas office in Teheran and ongoing Iranian weapon shipments for Hizbollah, the prospects for such disruptive activities remains serious.[57] The particularly violent clashes between Hizbollah and Israel that rocked southern Lebanon in late July 1993 are a classic example. Iran not only vocally supported the Hizbollah militants but also supplied them with planeloads of arms.[58] U.S. Secretary of State Christopher managed to broker a cease-fire and after an energetic bout of shuttle diplomacy secured commitments from the regional states to continue the peace talks.[59] Iran may try to foment similar clashes to derail the process and undermine support for the Israeli-Palestinian agreement.

Direct Iranian leadership of a rejuvenated rejectionist front is an alternative that appears possible given Iran's negative response to the surprising turn of recent events. Iranian leaders have suggested that they are capable of leading the forces opposed to the Israel-PLO agreement and the entire Madrid process. After the agreement was initiated, Rafsanjani referred to the event as "the most degrading times for the Islamic holy war in Palestine." Iranian officials have called the agreement "a stain of shame" for Arabs and Muslims and derided it as irrelevant paper signed by a few men.[60] Rather than supporting the agreement or even ameliorating their criticism of the negotiated approach, Iranian leaders have used the signing as an opportunity to step up their attacks on the peace process, though there is little evidence such rhetoric has had any significant negative impact. The most troubling role Iran plays is continuing support, including funds, for Hamas.

In the wake of the Israeli-Palestinian agreement, Iranian rejectionism carries greater risks for Iran's foreign and economic relations, especially the potential for friction with Europe and Japan. Both have been far more willing to deal with Iran than the United States has been. With their strong support for the Israel-PLO agreement, Europe and Japan are more likely to heed U.S. calls for diminished ties with Iran and support rejection of Iranian requests for debt relief from the international financial institutions.

IRANIAN HUMAN RIGHTS ABUSES

Political oppression is common in the Islamic Republic. Peaceful opposition forces are at best treated with disdain by the government. Usually, significant dissent is dealt with harshly; arrest, imprisonment and torture are common features of the Iranian system. Executions for political crimes are not unusual. In the first six months of 1992, the U.N. Commission on Human Rights estimated that sixty-six Iranians were executed for political transgressions. While the purges of government opponents and decimation of political adversaries have subsided compared with the early days of the revolution, such human rights abuses still occur. Political dissent and nonviolent opposition to government activities are still considered punishable offenses.

Once arrested, Iranians are frequently denied basic rights within the judicial system. Trials often take place in secret. Though the constitution theoretically guarantees representation by counsel, Amnesty International reports that most of the accused lack legal representation. Various American and international organizations condemn the lack of fairness in Iranian revolutionary courts. They claim that by international legal standards Iranian courts cannot be considered balanced. Political dissidents and other defendants lack basic legal rights in the Iranian system.

Religious persecution, especially of religions like Baha'i, is significant and deadly. Iran rejects Baha'i, considering it as a "misguided sect."[1] The Baha'i number some 300,000 to 350,000 and are routinely abused, arrested and killed. The U.N. Commission estimated in late 1992 that nearly 200 Baha'is have been killed since the revolutionary takeover. No aspect of Baha'i life is safe from governmental interference. The Iranian government rejects Baha'i marriages, blocks higher education opportunities and confiscates Baha'i property. Even prominent Baha'is are not safe from the government's reach, as demonstrated by the 1992 execution of Bahman Samandari. Repression of the Baha'is is consistent, a clear violation of their human rights and all too often has deadly consequences.

At least by the measure of Western standards, women are marginalized in Iranian society. Some categories of employment and education are restricted. Women are barred from studying a number of specific disciplines, including engineering and agriculture. Only men may be judges in Iran. Issues of dress are also controversial; strict dress codes tied to Islamic law have led to condemnation and harassment of inappropriately dressed women.

Iran's defenders refer to a number of qualifying factors to suggest a different understanding of Iran's human rights behavior. They assert that when compared with Saudi Arabia, Kuwait, Iraq or other states in the region, Iranian policy is better on human rights.[2] The U.S. State Department reports, they allege, are biased and favor U.S. client states in the region. In addition, they note, such simplistic judgments about the Iranian system fail to account for differences between Western standards and Islamic sensibilities. They see the human rights assessments of the United States or United Nations, made according to Western yardsticks, as creating artificial problems that would not exist if Iran were seen within the proper framework, an Islamic republic. Both the method of assessing Iranian society and an effective understanding of individual events within it depend on variations in Islamic and Western societies. (For more detail on Iran's human rights record, see Appendix III.)

THE RUSHDIE CASE

Iran's most glaring example of clerical extremism remains the fatwa (religious edict) sentencing the British author Salman Rushdie to death for the publication of his book, *The Satanic Verses*. Anyone who died ridding the world of Rushdie, Ayatollah Khomenei said, was a martyr who would go directly to heaven. In November 1992, the reward for killing Rushdie was increased to $3 million from the original $2 million. Iranian government officials persist in calling the fatwa irrevocable. "We have nothing new to tell you. Our position is what it used to be," declared Iran's foreign minister after the last Majles election.[3]

The affair continues to strain Iran's relations with Britain and more generally, with the West. Maintaining a death warrant on a British author for the publication of a work outside of Iran is totally irreconcilable with basic Western respect for individual human rights. (Appendix II gives greater detail on the case.)

UNITED STATES POLICY: RECOMMENDATIONS

The enmity between the United States and Iran is deep. Both countries have fundamentally different perspectives and remain highly suspicious of each other even while continuing to expand trade relations. The Clinton administration is often at odds with its European allies, Japan and Russia as to the most effective way to influence Iranian behavior. Within Iran foreign policy is hostage to bitterly divisive conflicts among the leadership. Most of Iran's immediate neighbors wish to improve relations but are nervous about the regime's geopolitical and ideological outreach. The Arab Gulf countries, in particular, regard the United States as their best guarantor against Iranian military adventurism. While Iran's military programs are potentially threatening to the United States and regional security, views differ as to when the threats will become a reality. Iranian support for international terrorism and subversion and its continued human rights abuses are well documented.

Iran is a key player in the Persian Gulf, a region of vital importance to the United States. Yet American policy toward the region remains enigmatic. Aside from agreement on the enduring importance of Gulf oil, there are strong differences of opinion on how to deal with the Gulf Arabs and Iraq, as well as Iran. For instance there is ambivalence on how far the United States should press for greater democracy and human rights when dealing with strategic allies such as Saudi Arabia or Oman, both of whom have poor records on these matters. Similarly there is ambiguity as to whether it is in U.S. interests to continue to support Iraq's territorial integrity and central control by Baghdad rather than work for a looser Iraqi confederation with autonomy for the Kurds and possibly the Marsh Arabs. These dilemmas are part of the changing and complex environment of the Persian Gulf, a region that is *terra incognita* for even the most experienced foreign policy planner. This environment, in turn, is hostage to much larger apprehensions about the regional and global impact of the breakup of the Soviet Union and the confusion and chaos it has left in its wake. In this new environment the United States has found it difficult to articulate a coherent policy for Europe, a region it knows well. It hardly surprising that a comprehensive American policy in the Persian Gulf remains elusive where the vicissitudes are every bit as great as in Europe.

Both the animosity of the regime and the uncertainties of the country and the area limit United States choices in formulating a realistic policy toward Iran. Moreover, given the experience of his three predecessors' disastrous encounters with the Iranian regime, it would be politically

difficult and risky for President Clinton to advocate any changes in U.S.
policy involving significant concessions. A tougher, more confrontational
policy to try to bring down the Islamic regime may be appealing to those
who believe radical mullahs represent a regional as well as global challenge to stability. However in the absence of further major Iranian transgressions such a policy will be undermined by its rejection by key allies.

Given these constraints what should be the goals of American policy?
The most important are changes in Iranian behavior on four key issues:
its efforts to obtain nuclear weapons; its opposition to the Arab-Israel
peace process; its support for terrorism and subversion of neighbors; its
human rights abuses. In pursuing these goals the United States should
use tough unilateral and multilateral pressures on Iran but should acknowledge the legitimacy of the Islamic regime and be prepared for talks
with its leaders at any time without any conditions. It should offer Iran
the prospects for normal relations, particularly better economic ties, if
progress is made resolving the most serious points of contention, especially those relating to nuclear weapons, subversion and terrorism.

In many ways these goals mirror those enunciated by Clinton's national
security advisor, Anthony Lake, in his *Foreign Affairs* essay. Clinton's policy calls for Iran to abandon its radical agenda but also engage in a dialogue with the United States. This approach puts the onus on Iran's leaders to respond.

Nevertheless the Clinton policy has weaknesses. It still relies almost entirely on negative initiatives to influence Iranian behavior: military deterrence, strict restrictions on technology transfers and denial of Iran's requests for international economic assistance. The present policy offers
Iran few, if any, positive inducements, or "carrots," to change its ways.
Furthermore, though the harsh and often counterproductive rhetoric toward Iran has been toned down, the administration's failure to reach a
consensus with allies as to the best way to stop Iran's unacceptable behavior makes its achievement virtually impossible.

Most strange, however, is the administration's silence on how to deal
with Russia. Unlike this study which highlights the important role of Russia in Persian Gulf geopolitics, Lake's analysis contains not one word on
Russia! This is a very significant omission. Without Soviet, and then Russian, cooperation recent favorable developments in the Middle East would
have been unlikely, including Syria's decision to mend relations with the
moderate Arabs, the American success during Desert Shield and Desert
Storm, and the Madrid Conference on Arab-Israeli peace. More ominous,
in the future a less cooperative Russia or, in extremis, a hostile Russia,

could undermine many American goals in the Gulf including those relating to military security. Russia has its own strategic agenda in the region and seeks markets for its arms industry, including sales to Iran and, if Saddam Hussein is ousted, to Iraq.

To base policy on this narrow approach in such a volatile and vital region runs the risk that the United States will be ignored by allies, denied the opportunity to talk to Iranian leaders, and possibly bypassed on key regional decisions that have great impact on American interests. It is therefore important that the United States present a concept of how relations might improve if Iran changes its most radical policies, what positive, reciprocal, steps the U.S. would be prepared to take to help bring this about, and how such actions could, and should, be coordinated with allies.

Such an approach makes sense in the post-Cold War world. Old paradigms are being discarded with amazing speed, the Israeli-PLO dialogue being the latest surprising drama. Of course, constructive engagement with Iran for its own sake will not assure better relations and long term stability. However as the world's only superpower and given the stakes involved in the Gulf, the United States cannot afford to adopt a reactive and rhetorical role. The United States, by virtue of its military presence, continues to wield an impressive stick over Iran and its rejectionist allies, but more than sticks are needed to avoid dangerous confrontation with such an important adversary.

The immediate problem is that so long as Iran's leaders believe the regime derives legitimacy from adopting a strident, rejecting posture toward Western interests in the Persian Gulf and Middle East, there will be no major changes in U.S.-Iranian relations. Iranian hostility will likely continue so long as the radicals bitterly oppose any dealings with the United States and others, including some pragmatists, believe that compromise with the United States could threaten the survival of the Islamic regime since it requires Iran to make key concessions. They fear the so-called Gorbachev syndrome. That is to say the Islamic Republic would appease the West, adopt more open policies on economic reform, foreign policy and human rights and sooner or later the ideological underpinnings of the revolution would be discarded or diluted beyond recognition. The leadership could then be replaced by reformed revolutionaries and end the same way Gorbachev and his supporters did—out of power and politically discredited.

In the face of continued Iranian intransigence on the main issues of contention the only way to pursue U.S. goals is to work in close coordination with allies to adopt a series of measures designed to put concerted pressure on the regime. This will not be easy. Unless the United States shows determined leadership and is prepared to make a strong case for unified action while articulating a better strategic vision of its Middle East policies, the allies are likely to balk at further tough action against Iran. The U.S. goal must be to present the regime with a united front if it continues to pursue policies inimical to allied interests. Its leaders must be frequently informed, preferably by European allies, that their current policies guarantee that relations will not remain stable — they will deteriorate.

The nuclear issue is of paramount importance to the United States. An Iranian nuclear capability will radically alter the balance of power in the Middle East. It will increase the dangers of military confrontation since there will be strong pressures from many sources to prevent by any means, including military action, the deployment of an operational Iranian nuclear force. Although there is a consensus on this issue among the allies, more must be done. Allied intelligence agencies should continue to concentrate on developing a much better capability to detect and, if necessary, prevent efforts by Iran to procure nuclear items and nuclear know-how on the black market. This takes on greater urgency given the chaos and confusion in the former Soviet Union and Iran's close proximity to the region.

Given the poor performance of the International Atomic Energy Agency (IAEA) in detecting nuclear cheating by Iraq and North Korea, who were signatories of the Non-Proliferation Treaty (NPT), it would be unwise to rely solely on this agency to assure Iranian compliance with its treaty obligations. Nevertheless, the IAEA must be given full backing by the United States in the hope that its future vigilance will be much improved. It must be urged to persuade Iran that it is in its own interests to continue to permit more intrusive inspections of its nuclear facilities. If Iran does not cooperate, other measures, including sanctions will have to be considered. The IAEA will be in a stronger position to assure Iran's cooperation on this matter if there is convincing evidence that Iraq's capability to assemble or produce nuclear weapons-grade material has been permanently halted. In order to persuade supplier countries such as Russia, China, Europe and Japan to tighten export controls on technologies related to nuclear weapons development, a review of all technology transfer issues will be necessary. This will likely have to be coupled with a less dogmatic U.S. position on conventional arms sales to Iran, which bring much-needed hard currency to Russia and China.

The second priority must be to neutralize Iran's opposition to the Arab-Israeli peace process. While Iran could, in theory, use the breakthrough in the peace process to improve relations with the United States and, in addition, accept Israel's right to exist, its leaders have done the opposite and are now serving as the locus of the rejectionist front. A third and related goal concerns Iran's support for anti-government groups, including terrorists, in the Middle East and its continued assassination campaign against its opponents outside the region.

The United States, together with Europe, and hopefully Japan and Russia, must communicate more strongly and more unequivocally to the Iranian leadership that these activities will cause it to pay a heavy price. Iranian requests for better terms for repaying its debts and for obtaining additional loans from the international financial institutions should be made conditional on changed behavior. Iranian involvement in specific terrorist activities and efforts to subvert pro-Western regimes should be more widely publicized by the U.S. government, as should actions by European countries such as France to appease Iran on these matters. In this regard a few successful counterterrorist operations against Iranian-sponsored terrorist groups would send an appropriate message. In addition, allied pressures on Sudan and Syria to stop providing sanctuaries and bases for Iranian-backed extremist groups should be increased. Syria should not be allowed to use its more cooperative role in the Arab-Israel peace negotiations to absolve it of responsibility for harboring terrorists. A U.N. Security Council resolution supporting the Israeli-Palestinian agreement should be sought—this would further isolate Iran and the rejectionists.

Last on the immediate agenda, the United States must continue to spotlight specific Iranian human rights abuses. The removal of the death sentence on Salman Rushdie and ending the persecution of the Baha'i should be priority goals because they are very visible steps the Iranian regime could take to improve its bad reputation. On the Rushdie case, the United States should seek cooperation with Russia, whose diplomats believe that Islamic fora can be used to persuade Iran to reverse the death sentence.

In parallel, and assuming Iran continues nuclear, terrorist and subversive activities including intimidation of its neighbors, the United States will need to strengthen its military presence in the Persian Gulf. Though reliance on military power to secure U.S. interests in the Gulf carries considerable risks, the United States has no alternative but to bolster its military capabilities in the region, including strengthening those of local allies. The United States should press ahead with bilateral defense agreements with the Arab Gulf countries and intensify joint military training and preparedness, including prepositioning of equipment.

There is no guarantee that this menu of tough actions will be sufficient to persuade Iran to change its behavior even if key allies are in concurrence. However until they have been presented with a more concerted allied approach, more extreme policies advocating either more carrots or more sticks are not practical, however appealing they may be to their advocates.

If Iran's leaders reach the conclusion that their current policies are counterproductive or need modification, or even if they just wish to talk and explain their policies in a dialogue, a second policy agenda should come into play. In these circumstances one can anticipate a great deal of tactical maneuvering by the two sides to determine what items should go to the top of the agenda. Should the United States insist that some progress be made on resolving the most controversial issues *before* other items could be discussed? Alternatively, should the talks begin with less contentious items to see if, in the spirit of compromise and accommodation, a constructive dialogue on the tough questions could eventually begin? These questions will only be resolved when the two countries begin preliminary discussions. In view of the bad experiences of past dealings with the regime, U.S. negotiators should be insistent that *all* issues be on the agenda and that consideration of those items of most concern to the United States not be held hostage to progress on resolving other problems high on Iran's list such as return of appropriated assets.

Among the issues on the second agenda, one of the most important for the United States concerns Iran's conventional rearmament program and what to do about it. Prior to any dialogue with the Iranians, there should be agreement within the U.S. government as to those elements of the program that it regards as most threatening and those that are less dangerous. This will not be an easy exercise since, in theory, all components of a country's conventional forces, including so-called "defensive" and "offensive" forces, contribute to its overall capabilities. That said, though the United States cannot prevent Iran from rearming its conventional forces, it should make clear that if Iran develops a major sea-denial capability, including a modern submarine fleet, a large antiship missile force and long-range attack aircraft squadrons, it will be treated as a major threat and contingency planning for U.S. military action will be intensified. The United States should therefore vigorously seek to prevent or limit the sale of certain classes of conventional arms to Iran. Since Iran is unlikely to limit its arms requests at American bidding, a careful and diplomatic approach to Iran's arms suppliers is necessary to persuade countries like Russia and China to show restraint, especially in view of continued major U.S. arms sales to the GCC countries. This approach would entail some relaxation of U.S. concerns about Iran's purchases of small arms, artillery, armor, maritime patrol capabilities, air defense and communications systems, even though these force components have potentially offensive operational capabilities. To make conventional arms restraint more palatable to Iran, the United States must champion a continued embargo on conventional arms sales to Iraq, *even if* Iraq is in compliance with the key U.N. resolutions that imposed sanctions at the time of the Gulf War.

The future of Iraq is of great importance to both the United States and Iran. The two countries may differ on whether Saddam Hussein's continued control of Iraq has more benefits than costs, and both countries have different agendas as to what sort of regime they would like to see replace Saddam Hussein. For the time being they share common interests in wishing to keep Iraq weak without destroying its territorial integrity. Iran has to worry if Saddam were replaced by a pro-Western government. The United States would be concerned if a pro-Iranian Islamic regime emerged. Neither possibility is likely to happen soon. More likely, but equally serious from an Iranian perspective, is that sanctions against the current regime will be lifted. Saddam Hussein's power base would then be strengthened with access to substantial oil revenues. This would eventually permit the further rebuilding of his military forces and would further contribute to the depression of world oil prices. While the United States would welcome lower oil prices and Iran will not, both countries have reason to fear the enhancement of Iraqi military power. Mutual concern about Iraq may also extend to Saddam Hussein's barbaric treatment of the Marsh Arabs. The destruction of the marshes increases refugee pressures on Iran and strengthens Saddam's ability to retain control over southern Iraq.

However there are strong indications that the two countries have different attitudes towards the Kurdish enclave that has been established in northern Iraq. Kurdish autonomy in the north should be an American goal and should be advocated, hopefully with the blessing of Turkey. Iran, on the other hand, has expressed concern that the enclave has become "another Israel" in the region and feels threatened by the breakup of Iraq into independent ethnic regions. If the United States and Iran were to discuss their mutual concerns about Iraq they are most likely to find some common ground concerning Iran's humanitarian role in helping the Marsh Arabs and the dangers of a rearmed Saddam Hussein. On this point most Arab countries would probably concur.

In principle, the United States and Iran share some common interests in the Caucasus, Central Asia and the Balkans. While the United States would not wish to see a proliferation of extremist Muslim regimes, neither country benefits from instability in these regions. Both Iran and Turkey wish to see a stable relationship between Armenia and Azerbaijan; so does the United States, who would like to avoid a dispute with Turkey over Armenia. In Central Asia neither the United States nor Iran wish to see escalating violence which undermines economic opportunities and assures continued Russian military presence in the former Soviet republics. Concerning the Balkans, both countries share interests in wishing to protect the Muslim population and end the Bosnian crisis. Both wish to see the U.N. arms embargo on Bosnia lifted and Iran would probably support allied air strikes against Serbian forces. All these issues would be natural agenda items if Iran and the United States engage in dialogue.

On economic issues, the United States should continue to state that it is eventually prepared to resolve all outstanding questions relating to appropriated assets and establish a normal trading relationship with the Iranian regime. This could include the sale of commercial jet airliners and a number of high-technology items currently proscribed by executive order or public laws. It should also seek to work with the regime to resolve the outstanding geographical claims between Iran and its Arab neighbors including the Shatt al-Arab, Abu Musa and demarcation disputes for offshore exploration and drilling and extraction rights.

There are a number of other issues that have importance for Iran and are of interest to the United States. Iran believes that it has legitimate grievances against the United States, especially regarding its treatment during the Iran-Iraq War. While the U.S. tilt toward Iraq during the Iran-Iraq War was justified and Iran's behavior over American hostages disgraceful, the failure of the United States and the West to seriously condemn Iraq for its massive use of chemical weapons has made it difficult to convince Iranians that limitations on all weapons of mass destruction is high on the American agenda. Although Iran is unlikely to join any regional forum on security and arms control in the near term, the reality is that without Iranian participation regional arms control will be impossible to achieve. The United States should acknowledge this reality and express the hope that some day Iran would be part of a Persian Gulf security regime. The United States should continue to stress that Islamic fundamentalism is a complex phenomenon and that not all Islamic radical movements are inimical to Western interests. To this extent a greater effort must be made to distinguish between terrorists acting in the name of Islam whose behavior cannot be tolerated and Islamic fundamentalists who are critical of Western secularism and many of its values but who oppose the use of violence.

In conclusion, while the United States should support some sort of constructive engagement with Iran, the prospects for an early dialogue are slim. Indeed, to change Iranian behavior to the point where its leaders will see that such a dialogue is in their interests will require the close co-operation of allies and may mean intensified economic and political pressures on the Teheran regime. If U.S.-Iranian talks begin there should be no expectations of early progress, even on the issues where there is common ground. Rather, a dialogue should be regarded as the beginning of a long process to restore normalcy to relations between two countries too important to ignore each other.

APPENDICES

IRAN'S GEOGRAPHY AND THE LOGISTICS OF CENTRAL ASIA

Iran's geography, topography and demographics are key to understanding Iran's importance in the Middle East and Central Asia. With a total area of 1,648,000 square kilometers (636,300 square miles), Iran is far larger than any West European country. Iran ranks seventeenth among the world's nations in geographic mass while its population is in the top twenty-five with close to 60 million people. Iran's population is twice that of all the Gulf Cooperation Council (GCC) countries combined. Physically, the country is bounded by Azerbaijan, Armenia and Turkmenistan to the north; Turkey and Iraq to the west; and Afghanistan and Pakistan to the east. Of the country's 7,192 kilometer (4,470 mile) boundary 3,180 kilometers (1,972 miles) is sea coast, including littorals along the Caspian Sea, the Persian Gulf and the Gulf of Oman.

The terrain is generally mountainous. Massive, heavily eroded mountain ranges surround a largely arid basin and, in contrast to the coastal areas, most of the country is more than 457 m (1,500 feet) above sea level. The Elburz Mountains extend along the coast of the Caspian Sea into Khorasan, while the Zagros range runs along the western border from Armenia to the Persian Gulf and into Baluchistan. At 5,671 m (18,606 feet), the highest mountain in the country is an old volcanic peak called Mount Damavand.[1]

Climates range from subtropical to subpolar. Altitude, latitude, maritime influences, seasonal winds and proximity to mountain ranges or deserts play an important role in fluctuating temperatures, which vary from 55 °C (131 °F) in Khuzistan in the summer, to -37 °C (-35°F) in Azerbaijan province in the winter. Rainfall also varies from less than 5 cms (2 inches) in Baluchistan in the southeast to 198 cms (78 inches) in the Caspian region, though the annual average is about 41 cms (16 inches).

Iran contains 10 percent of the world's known oil reserves in the southwest region of the country where most exploration and production takes place. Before the revolution, Iran was the world's fourth largest producer of petroleum at 5.6 million barrels per day, the peak in 1976.[2] Iran has not approached this level in recent years. In 1993, Iran produced between 3.3 million and 3.7 million barrels per day.[3]

Unlike the economies of the GCC, mainly based on a single commodity, Iran also has the world's second largest reserve of natural gas, as well as other minerals.[4] Natural gas is mostly found in the Elburz mountains and in Khorasan; the state-owned system, IGAT, is one of the Middle East's largest gas lines. Besides natural gas, other mineral resources, such

---

Transportation Routes: Iran, Caucasus and Central Asia

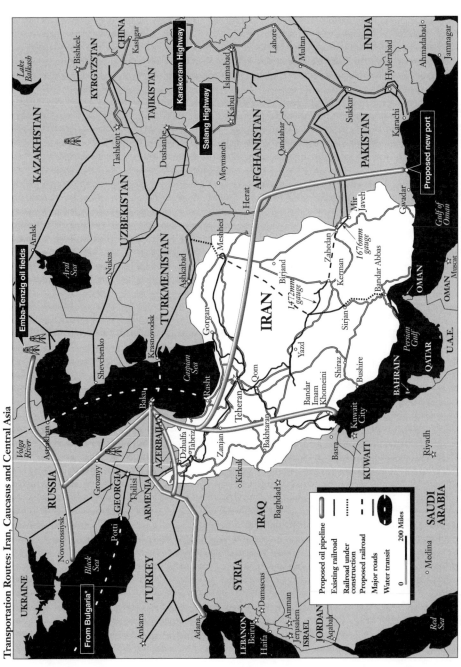

* Goods would move by truck between Georgia and Iran.   Representations of proposed routes are not intended to delineate the exact pathway.   SOURCE: Carnegie Endowment research

as coal, copper, zinc and lead, are scattered throughout the country, but have been exploited to a lesser extent.

In the absence of adequate irrigation, the harsh topography and extremes of climate hamper agricultural productivity. Less than 10 percent of the agricultural land in rural areas is under cultivation; 9.8 percent of Iranian farmland is irrigated.[5] The land that is not irrigated is largely devoted to dry farming and animal husbandry. As a result of underdevelopment, neglect and difficult geographic conditions, and despite a largely agrarian society, agricultural activities provide a relatively small part of the gross domestic product. Illustrating the current state of affairs is the unofficial estimate that between 1979 and 1991, employment in the agriculture sector increased by about 10 percent, while service sector jobs nearly doubled.[6]

Road and Rail Logistics

Iran possesses an extensive road and rail network of varying quality. With the breakup of the Soviet Union, a flurry of new proposals have been suggested to strengthen the Iranian transportation system. A review of both the existing infrastructure and the proposed additions is helpful in evaluating the possibility of Iran's evolution as a regional trade hub.

The Existing Network

Iran is linked to all of its neighbors by road (see map). It is unclear whether all of these can function as major trade routes. Iran has made one advance by adding official border posts. In April 1992, border crossings were opened at Bajgiran and Istgah-e Pol to facilitate the flow of passengers and goods between Iran and Turkmenistan. According to 1989 figures, Iran has 490 kilometers (304 miles) of highways, 18,044 kilometers (11,213 miles) of paved main roads and 33,275 kilometers (20,677 miles) of paved feeder roads.[7] Other sources suggest a total of 42,694 kilometers (26,530 miles) of paved surfaces.[8]

Whatever the total, a few principal roads stand out. A major highway runs the length of Iran's eastern border regions and connects Pakistan and Turkmenistan via Iran. The road is connected to Pakistan via Zahedan and may figure in Pakistan's hopes for greater trade with Central Asia. The road runs to Chah Bahar, on the Gulf, and north to Ashkabad in Turkmenistan. According to maps produced by the California-based map company Map Link, the entire highway, except for the final stretch from Meshed to Ashkabad, is a "most important road" (MIR).[9] Another paved highway runs from Bazargan on the Turkish border to Afghanistan, a distance of 2,089 kilometers (1,298 miles).[10] A third highway runs east-west from Iraq to Mir Javeh; when fully operational, it will cover approximately 2500 kilometers (1,554 miles). Map Link classified both highways as MIRs. In September, 1992, Iran and Kazakhstan inaugurated a new transit route.[11]

Several smaller roads are notable. Meshed, which is connected by road (MIR) to Bandar Abbas on the Gulf, is a short trip from Ashkabad, although the ride involves some secondary roads. From Ashkabad there are roads to such key eastern cities of Central Asia as Tashkent and Dushanbe. Meshed is also linked by MIRs to Teheran, Tabriz and the southern shores of the Caspian Sea. In northwestern Iran, roads (MIRS and connecting roads) connect Teheran and Tabriz with Baku, Azerbaijan.

From the a transnational perspective, important roads (MIRs) go from Iran to Pakistan, Afghanistan (Herat), Turkey and Iraq. Connecting roads (CR), roads of slightly lesser quality than MIRs, link Iran to Azerbaijan and Nakichevan. The size of roads between Iran and Turkmenistan varies. One road near the Caspian Sea is a connecting road. Those closer to Meshed are secondary roads that eventually join important roads (MIRs) that run to Ashkabad. No road, not even a secondary one, crosses the Iran-Armenia border.

A floating bridge connected Armenia and Iran across the river Arkas in the Nurdowr region in Iran. The bridge was 100 meters (328 feet) long and the first one to be constructed since the independence of the former Soviet republics.[12] This bridge may have mitigated the impact of the absence of quality roads between the two countries. It was washed away in the April 1993 floods but was being rebuilt as of August 1993.[13]

The rail system centers on Teheran. Rail lines run south, east and west from the capital. Despite the significant lengths of rail that exist, a few key sections are missing. The total length of rail in place was 4,821 kilometers (2,996 miles) as of November 1992. Iran expects to add another 1,000 kilometers (621 miles) by March 1994.[14]

Traveling south from Teheran, there are two major lines. One links Teheran to Kerman via Qom and Yazd. A line from Kerman to Zahedan, a border town connected to the Pakistani rail network, has been proposed or, according to some sources, is already under construction.[15] The northern section of a rail line from Bafq, which sits on the Teheran-Kerman line, to Bandar Abbas on the Persian Gulf, was opened in 1990; the southern section is under construction and due to be completed in 1994 or 1995.[16] A second major line south of Teheran connects Qom to Korramshahr and Bandar Imam Khomeini via Ahvaz and Defzul. It is unclear whether this line is still intact since it winds close to the Iraqi border and may have come under attack during the Iran-Iraq War.

The rail lines heading east from Teheran are key routes in the context of Central Asia. The railroad links Teheran to Meshed but stops short of the Turkmen border. The same line forks at Gayershabad and goes on to Gorgan via Qa'emshahr, located near the Caspian Sea. To the west, Teheran is linked to both Turkey and the Caucasus region. The main line links Teheran to Van, Turkey via Tabriz. That line splits at Sawfyan and links Iran to the Caucasus through Nakichevan, via Dzhulfa in Iran. Despite the Armenian-Azerbaijani conflict, Iran's rail connection to the Caucasus appears to be operational.

Thus, Iran's only international rail links are with Turkey and Armenia/Azerbaijan. There are no direct rail links with Pakistan, Afghanistan or Turkmenistan. The only rail link with the Gulf runs to the ports of Korramnshahr and Bandar Imam Khomeini, the old Persian corridor, and is located in the Iran-Iraq War zone.

ADDITIONAL CONSTRUCTION AND PROPOSALS

In May 1992, Rafsanjani stressed the need to construct border roads to facilitate ground transport between the republics.[17] Iran, Georgia and Bulgaria signed an accord to build a road link from the Black Sea to Iran's northern border. A shipping line would transport cargo from the Bulgarian port of Burgas to the Georgian port of Potti on the eastern shore of the Black Sea. From there, goods would be transferred by truck to Iran's northern border.[18] In addition, a 1,700 kilometer (1,056 mile) road from Iran's Khorasan province to Turkmenistan, Uzbekistan and Tajikistan "will soon be operational" according to one Iranian official.[19]

Iran has lobbied the GCC and others for funding for rail links from Central Asia to the Gulf region. It claims that linking the two areas would bring an additional $20 billion of business to the region.[20] The Iranian plan of linking Central Asia to Europe through Iran was adopted in June 1992, by the U.N. Economic and Social Committee for Asia and the Pacific. The plan calls for the expansion of transport links along the old Silk Road by connecting the Mary-Tajan railway to Sarakhs and Meshed.[21]

Construction has begun on part of this proposal, a line that would connect Meshed to Sarakhs on the Turkmen border. In February 1993 the Islamic Republic News Agency reported "rapid progress" in the building of this line.[22] Turkmenistan is working to extend this line from Sarakhs to the Mary-Tajan line. Reports from June 1993 estimated that between 10 and 20 percent of the line was complete. The completion date for the entire project is between March 1996 and March 1997.[23] The extension would link Iran to the entire Central Asian rail network. With a completed line from Kerman to Zahedan, the Meshed-Sarakhs-Mary line would also link Pakistan to Central Asia via rail, though rather indirectly; this situation could improve if a direct Meshed–Bafq line were built in the late 1990s, as has been proposed.[24] Zahedan is connected by larger gauge track to Pakistan than is used on the rest of the Iranian rail network, but this would not prevent the linkage of the two lines. The connection of Bafq to the large Persian Gulf port of Bandar Abbas, anticipated in 1994 or 1995, also increases the appeal of this transit route.

Transit and trade negotiations are underway to link Iran's Caspian ports to other waterways. Iranian ships could eventually have transit facilities via the Volga River network enabling them to reach northern European and other waters. The other four countries that share the Caspian with Iran are Turkmenistan, Kazakhstan, the Russian Federation and Azerbaijan. Currently ships run between Baku and Krasnovodsk.[25]

PROPOSED PIPELINE ROUTES

Pipeline routes have become a major topic of proposed expansion and competition. Many of the Central Asian and Caucasus states have valuable oil and natural gas reserves but lack suitable means of export. Iran had urged Azerbaijan to send oil southward through Iran to the Persian Gulf. But in March 1993, the Azerbaijani government agreed to a pipeline proposal to export its oil through Turkey via Armenia, Iran or Georgia. Turkey is also interested in transporting Turkmenistan's natural gas and Kazakhstan's oil from the Tengiz fields. Iran and Turkmenistan have held talks concerning a natural gas pipeline, and other economic and transport issues as well. Russia may be able to offer a route for oil and gas from the Tengiz fields by constructing a pipeline to the Black Sea. Either of the two proposed Azerbaijani routes could also help move Kazakh oil. Another option would send the pipeline east toward Afghanistan to a Pakistani port on the Arabian Sea. In a separate, smaller venture, Iran will probably supply Armenia with gas through a new pipeline.[26]

TURKEY, PAKISTAN AND CENTRAL ASIA

Turkey's geographic location is a difficult one from which to exploit Central Asian markets. Most of its eastern border is shared with Iran and Armenia, neither of which is any great friend of the Turkish state. Turkey is connected to Iran by road and rail. To the extent that both countries are willing, Turkey could use these connections to reach Azerbaijan and, though more distant, Central Asia. Former Turkish President Turgut Ozal cited rail connections through Iran to Turkmenistan as one possible trade route. Among other factors, this is contingent on completing the rail line from Meshed to Sarakhs.

A second and shorter trade option involves the Caspian Sea. Currently, a ferry runs from Baku to Krasnovodsk, Turkmenistan on the eastern shore of the Caspian. Krasnovodsk is connected to Ashkabad by road and rail; the ferry can accomodate one freight train. President Ozal proposed using links by rail, road or a combination to Baku as a major trade route. Although small rail lines connect Turkey with Baku, they traverse Armenia. The ongoing Armenian-Azerbaijani conflict and Turkey's general reluctance to cooperate with Armenia make this option undesirable. This route could probably be circumvented by traveling via Georgia (there is a rail line from Batumi on the Black Sea to Baku) or Iran. Fighting in Georgia adds an additional complication.

There are no rail links between Pakistan and Central Asia. The British built no railroads to the north for fear of Russian expansionism; they wanted no rail lines that the Russians could use to transport troops toward India. Northern Pakistan is very mountainous and building a rail link in this area (for example from Mazar-i-Sharif in northern Afghanistan to Islamabad) would be difficult.

Pakistan has four major roads leading to Central Asia. All eventually lead to the port at Karachi, but each has some major drawback precluding cost-effective use or preventing its use altogether. Both the road through Afghanistan, via Kabul on the Salang highway, to Dushanbe, Tajikistan, and the road through Afghanistan, via Kandahar and Herat, to Ashkabad, Turkmenistan, are unsafe as a result of the civil war in Afghanistan. The road through China, via Kashgar on the Karakoram highway, to Bishkek, Kyrgyzstan and Tashkent, Uzbekistan, is a mountainous route unsuited to heavy trade. Lastly, the route through Iran to Ashkabad, Turkmenistan is very long and depends on the goodwill of an economic competitor, Iran, in Central Asia.

PROSPECTS FOR IRAN IN CENTRAL ASIA

By virtue of its location, the Islamic Republic has logistical advantages over its neighbors vis-a-vis trade with Central Asia. Political and economic ties with Turkmenistan provide a launching pad for the exchange of goods and services with all the Central Asian states. Roads are one obvious and basic method to move goods. Railroads could play a greater role if Iran completes the rail lines to Turkmenistan, Pakistan and Bandar Abbas. With these three lines, Iran would be linked to all of Central Asia; Iran could also serve as a crossing point for trade with Europe via Turkey. Providing access to a Persian Gulf port like Bandar Abbas would also bolster the Iranian share of regional trade.

Despite these possibilities, severe constraints persist. Iran's economy affords little capital to invest in transport improvements. Foreign financial backers are needed, yet Iran's political stance with regard to the United States and the GCC seemingly precludes any backing without changes in Iranian behavior and policies. In addition, Central Asia's transportation network is oriented north towards Moscow, not southward. While there is room for other economic partners, Russia will likely remain the major player for many years to come.

Beyond Iran's prime geographic location, the Iranian government has the advantage of an unobstructed path to Central Asia. Military conflicts in Afghanistan, Armenia, Azerbaijan, Tajikistan and Georgia hamper Turkish and Pakistani efforts at trade expansion. With a few investments in crucial rail lines, Iran will be able to offer a markedly better route for goods. Relations with the border state of Turkmenistan are already cordial; if Iran can muster greater investment in infrastructure and transport systems, its prospects of deriving economic benefits from Central Asia are good. Yet given the current state of the Iranian economy and its debtor status in the world financial institutions, it is unlikely that Iran can afford such an investment anytime soon. However, if the Iranian regime were to become more stable, over time it could become the key Middle East state linking Central Asia with the rest of the world.

THE RUSHDIE AFFAIR

Iran's death sentence against Salman Rushdie has pitted Iran's interpretation of Islam against the West's belief in the principle of national sovereignty and its commitment to the freedom of speech. As of late 1993, the issue remained in a deadlock. It has become an important element in the debate over future American policy toward Iran.

THE ORIGINS

On February 14, 1989, the Ayatollah Khomeini proclaimed the novel, *The Satanic Verses*, blasphemous to Islam and called for the author's death. Since that time, the novelist Salman Rushdie has lived in hiding under heavy police protection. The controversy had begun earlier and in different parts of the world. After the book's publication in Britain in late September 1988, Indian Muslims campaigned to have it banned from India because it offended their religion. They were successful, as India's minister of home affairs banned the book on October 5, 1988. Meanwhile, Muslims in England rallied to have the book banned but failed. To protest, they held book-burning demonstrations in Bolton on December 2, 1988 and in Bradford on January 14, 1989.

The uproar spread to South Africa where two anti-Apartheid institutions, the *Weekly Mail* and the Congress of South African Writers, had invited Rushdie to deliver a speech at a fall 1988 conference, they received numerous death threats and protests against the author. Under Muslim pressure, the government banned the book and the Congress withdrew its invitation one day before Rushdie was scheduled to arrive. The violence climaxed in Islamabad, Pakistan on February 12, 1989. A crowd of some 10,000 people marched to the American Cultural Center and burned the building. Five demonstrators were killed by police, and about a hundred were injured.

The early protests and violence that *The Satanic Verses* provoked were indicative of the potency of the issue to Muslims across the globe. Although the riots attracted attention, it took the Ayatollah Khomeini to propel the matter into a political confrontation between East and West.

THE EDICT AND THE RESPONSE

On February 14, 1989, Khomeini pronounced a fatwa (Islamic religious edict) against both Rushdie and his publishers:

> The author of the Satanic Verses book—which has
> been compiled, printed, and published in opposition
> to Islam, the Prophet, and the Koran—and all those

Prepared by Michelle Sieff

involved in its publication who were aware of its
content, are sentenced to death.[1]

Khomeini's edict met with support throughout Iran. To increase the incentive, the head of an Iranian charity organization offered a $1 million
bounty to the successful assailant. Members of the Iranian Parliament expressed "divine anger" at Rushdie and support for Khomeini. The Islamic
Revolutionary Guard Corps and Hizbollah, both sponsored by the Iranian
government, proclaimed their intention to assassinate Rushdie. By pro-
nouncing a death sentence on a Western citizen and his publishers, Khomeini transformed the Rushdie case into an international political incident.

The Muslim response to the edict differed at the official and popular
levels. Muslim governments withheld full support for Khomeini's fatwa.
At the Organization of the Islamic Conference meeting on March 13-16,
1989, the participating foreign ministers called for a ban on the book
though not the death of its author. Only the Libyan government backed
the Ayatollah's death edict. By contrast, Muslims on the street engaged in
anti-Rushdie violence and demonstrations, showing the edict's popular
support throughout India, Pakistan and elsewhere in the Muslim world.
Government leaders tried to avoid the issue. The most practical stance
adopted by virtually every leader with a sizable Muslim population was to
ban the book but say nothing of Rushdie.

The Western response was tepid. British Prime Minister Margaret
Thatcher said nothing about the fatwa for a full week and President
George Bush labelled the death sentence "offensive." The Canadian government temporarily banned imports of *The Satanic Verses*. The Japanese
government blandly stated "Mentioning or encouraging murder is not
something to be praised."[2] Finally, on February 20, the foreign ministers
of the European Community produced a statement condemning the
fatwa as "an unacceptable violation of the most elementary principles
...that govern relations among sovereign states."[3] At the same time they
recalled their heads of mission in Teheran for consultations and suspend-
ed exchanges of high-level official visits.

Yet the British government, which was the most affected by the Ayatollah's edict, refrained from breaking diplomatic relations, though it
withdrew all its personnel from Iran and demanded that all Iranian representatives leave London. In response, the Iranian government passed a
resolution on March 7 that threatened a complete break in relations if the
British government did not declare "its opposition to the unprincipled
stands against the world of Islam, the Islamic Republic of Iran, and the

contents of the anti-Islamic book, *The Satanic Verses.*"[4] The British tried to distance themselves from Rushdie in a public statement, but rejected Iran's other demands, legal prosecution of Rushdie, confiscation of copies of the book and an injunction against further publication. On March 7, Teheran broke off relations. In retaliation, the British expelled nine Iranian residents in the United Kingdom and closed the Iranian consulate in Hong Kong.

With the European Community's declaration and Britain's display of animosity towards Iran, it appeared that the West was resolute in its stance. Immediately afterward, the retreat from confrontation began.

One month after the E.C. ministers withdrew top diplomats from Iran, they acceded to Greek, Irish, and Italian pressure, and reinstated them. Britain made no attempt to restore relations with Teheran for a year. However, they took no further steps to have the fatwa rescinded and trade relations remained intact: The British continued to purchase Iranian crude oil, and the Iranians continued to purchase British products.

In 1990, the British moved toward restoring diplomatic relations with Teheran. In August, Foreign Minister Hurd made statements calling Islam "one of the world's great religions" and pointing out that the British government "had nothing to do with the publishing of *The Satanic Verses.*"[5] Finally, on September 28, Britain and Iran announced they were restoring diplomatic ties at all levels except the ambassadorial level. Justifying the resumption, the British government indicated that it was satisfied that Iran's leaders would no longer encourage Muslims to kill Rushdie. However, the death sentence was not repealed and Teheran could not guarantee that Muslims would not try to assassinate Rushdie on their own.[6]

Rushdie himself reinforced the general tendency to retreat and made attempts at reconciliation. In December 1990, he pledged not to authorize a paperback edition of his novel and stated that he would seek no more translations of the book. He disavowed passages in his book that question the authority of the Koran or the validity of Islam.[7] Rushdie's attempts were rebuffed, however, as the Ayatollah Khamenei responded by reiterating the irrevocable nature of the fatwa. Efforts at easing the confrontation proved futile. On July 3, 1991, the Italian translator of *The Satanic Verses* was stabbed in Milan and on July 13 the Japanese translator was found slain.

These incidents, the reaffirmation of the fatwa and the doubling of the bounty to $2 million, convinced Rushdie that appeasement was useless. He decided to take the initiative himself to resolve the issue and began venturing into public more frequently, giving readings and providing interviews, proclaiming his commitment to freedom of expression. In December 1991 at Columbia University, Rushdie delivered his first public speech since the fatwa had been issued.

On February 4, 1993, Rushdie, marked the approaching fourth anniversary of the death edict by emerging from his nomadic life of hiding to meet with Douglas Hogg, a British minister of state. This was only Rushdie's second meeting with a high-ranking British official in four years and the first held inside the Foreign Office itself. Rushdie pleaded for more aggressive support of his case. His efforts were rewarded: On February 14, British officials warned Iran that unless it retracted the death sentence, the two nations would be unable to resume full diplomatic relations.

The proclamation marked the first time that the British government explicitly linked relations with Iran to the abjuration of the fatwa. Iran's foreign minister, Ali Akbar Velayati, retorted that Western governments were wrong to link bilateral relations "to the destiny of this person."[8] Moreover, Iranian clerics reaffirmed the death sentence, and the bounty now amounting to more than $3 million.

Britain's new-found resolve on the Rushdie issue has brought the controversy to the fore once again. It has been met with calls in the American media for President Clinton to follow Britain's lead and assume a tougher stance against Teheran.[9] Prime Minister John Major agreed to meet with Rushdie, claiming that he is determined to fight this death sentence which he terms "outrageous."[10] The highly secretive encounter occurred on May 11, 1993; Rushdie attributed "great symbolic meaning" to the meeting and claimed it demonstrated Britain's willingness to internationalize the dispute.[11]

Besides the tougher British stand, in October 1992, the German Parliament issued a unanimous resolution making Iran legally responsible for anyone harmed by the fatwa and threatened sanctions in the event of an attack. It also abrogated a cultural agreement with Iran until the murder contract was rescinded. In the United States, White House Communications Director George Stephanopolous in early 1993 issued a statement saying: "We regard the fatwa as a violation of Mr. Rushdie's basic human rights, and therefore a violation of international law."[12] The renewed stalemate on the Rushdie issue was broken when the Norwegian publisher was shot on October 11, 1993.[13]

In November 1993, Rushdie met with President Clinton and Secretary of State Christopher. Iranian officials responded with strong denunciations of Clinton.[14]

REPORTS OF GOVERNMENTAL AND PRIVATE ORGANIZATIONS ON HUMAN RIGHTS IN IRAN

Numerous organizations have documented and criticized Iran's human rights record. The following appendix provides summaries of reports by major international and human rights organizations.[1]

UNITED NATIONS

Although various organs of the United Nations comment on human rights practices around the world, the U.N. Commission on Human Rights has been the most vocal on Iranian abuses. Two U.N. documents, one from January 1993 and the other from March 1993, are summarized. Since the publication of these U.N. documents in early 1993, the commission has continued to monitor the human rights situation in Iran. A November 1993 report by Reynaldo Galindo Pohl, special representative of the Commission on Human Rights on the situation of human rights in Iran, criticized Iranian human rights practices in several areas and concluded that "there is enough evidence to show that it is entirely proper for the human rights situation in the Islamic Republic of Iran to remain under international scrutiny."[2]

In a December 1993 resolution, the Third Committee of the U.N. General Assembly expressed its deep concern at continuing reports of Iranian human rights violations; the resolution passed 68 to 22 with 45 abstentions.[3]

SITUATION OF HUMAN RIGHTS IN THE ISLAMIC REPUBLIC OF IRAN[4]

January 28, 1993

Political executions and torture continue in Iran. The judicial system, notably the type of trials and the rights of the accused, do not meet international legal standards. The Baha'is continue to face arbitrary arrest and detention, discrimination in employment and education and a general lack of acceptance. A circular issued by the Supreme Revolutionary Cultural Council on February 25, 1991, defines government policy "such that their [Baha'i] progress and development shall be blocked." Women also face serious discrimination.

■ From January 1-July 31, 1992, there were 224 total executions, including "66 for political reasons."

■ The prohibition against torture "continues to be flouted." Methods include burning, beatings, blindfolds and reduced food rations.

■ "[C]ommon and political trials in the Islamic Republic of Iran continue to fall far short of internationally accepted standards for fair trials." Revolutionary Court trials are secret with summary proceedings, no de-

fense counsel, no presumption of innocence and no right to defense witnesses. Prisoner organizations are banned.

■ Arbitrary detention is used by government forces.

■ Constitutional provisions for freedom of press and freedom of expression are largely ignored.

■ Many political candidates have been excluded from elections by the
Council of Guardians. Often no explanation is given.

■ Women are barred from many fields in higher education including
engineering and agriculture. They cannot be judges. Only men can di-
vorce. Strict Islamic dress codes are enforced. Less resources and attention are focused on education for women; the female illiteracy rate is
higher.

■ "It has been reported that, since 1979, Baha'is have been systematically harassed and discriminated against for their religious beliefs and that
201 Baha'is have been killed; 15 other Baha'is have disappeared and are
presumed dead." Baha'is are subject to arbitrary arrest and detention.
They have been "systematically" denied access to higher education. Baha'i marriages and divorces are not legally recognized. Thousands have
been dismissed from government posts. They are not free to leave Iran
and have trouble getting passports.

■ "It was further reported that Baha'i-owned holy places, historical
sites, cemeteries, administrative centres and other assets, seized mostly in
1979, remain confiscated or have been destroyed."

■ The 1991 Supreme Revolutionary Cultural Council circular on the
Baha'i includes the following provisions:
- they shall not be expelled from the country;
- they shall not be detained, imprisoned or punished without reason;
- the government's treatment of them shall be such that their
  progress and development shall be blocked;
- Bahai's in school may not identify themselves as Baha'i;
- Baha'i students shall be expelled from universities;
- Baha'i religious activities and teaching shall be confronted by means
  of other religious activities and teaching; this includes an anti-
  Baha'i propaganda section of the Islamic Propaganda Organization;
- a plan shall be formulated to combat and destroy the cultural roots
  which this group has outside the country;
- they shall be permitted to lead a modest life; in most cases, they
  shall be allowed ration books, passports and work permits;
- employment shall be refused to persons identifying themselves as Baha'i;
- they shall also be denied positions of influence.

SITUATION OF HUMAN RIGHTS IN THE ISLAMIC REPUBLIC OF IRAN[5]

Resolution adopted March, 1993
On March 10, 1993, the U.N. Commission on Human Rights noted and expressed concern about continuing violations of human rights in Iran. The resolution referred to the Special Representative's interim report of November 13, 1992, and called on Iran to "investigate and rectify the human rights issues."[6]

■ "Expresses its concern more specifically at...the high number of executions, cases of torture and cruel, inhuman or degrading treatment or punishment, the standard of the administration of justice, the lack of guarantees of due process of law, discriminatory treatment of certain groups of citizens for reason of their religious beliefs, notably the Baha'is, and restrictions on the freedoms of expression, thought, opinion and the press and that...the situation of women leaves much to be desired;"
■ The use of the death penalty increased.
■ "Also expresses its grave concern that there are continuing threats to the life of a citizen of another state" [Salman Rushdie] with support from the Iranian government.
■ Regrets that Iran has not followed up on previous reports and has barred the U.N. Special Representative for more than a year.

U.S. DEPARTMENT OF STATE

The U.S. Department of State annually reviews the global human rights situation. Some observers have accused U.S. political allegiances of interfering with an objective evaluation of the state of human rights. The State Department report on Iran is partially based on U.N. reports.

COUNTRY REPORTS ON HUMAN RIGHTS PRACTICES FOR 1992[7]

February, 1993
Iranians lack many of the basic freedoms associated with a liberal democracy, including freedom of speech and press. Iranians do not retain the right to peacefully change their system of government. Baha'is, political opponents, workers and women suffer various levels of discrimination. Torture, arrest, detention and other repressive methods are commonly used by the government.

■ "Iran continues to be a major abuser of human rights, and there was no evidence of significant improvement in 1992."

■ Summary executions have been noted.

■ The use of torture is "widespread," including torture in detention and arbitrary brutalization of prisoners.

■ Arbitrary arrest, detention and exile are common tools used against the Baha'is and political offenders.

■ Repression of the freedoms of speech, press, assembly and association includes censorship, review of books before publication and limits on newspapers. "In practice, most independent organizations have either been banned, co-opted by the Government, or are moribund."

■ "By international standards, trials by revolutionary courts cannot be considered fair or public." Revolutionary courts have greater power than civil courts and cover political cases, narcotics cases and crimes against God. In revolutionary courts, it is rare to have counsel and the accused is unable to call defense witnesses or to appeal. These trials are usually short and often not public.

■ "The Government has continued to attack the Baha'i community as a front for political and espionage activities and prohibits the community from electing leaders or conducting religious activities." The Baha'is "may not teach their faith."

■ Citizens are denied the right to change their government. "Only supporters of the theocratic state are accepted" as political candidates.

■ There are "severe" restrictions on women and workers' rights. For women one issue of concern is strict dress codes; discrimination against women has increased since the revolution. Workers have no labor unions and are protected by weak labor laws.

HUMAN RIGHTS WATCH
Human Rights Watch is one of the well known, non-governmental international human rights organizations. It has several divisions, including Middle East Watch. Human Rights Watch also issues an annual report; the section on Iran is summarized below.

HUMAN RIGHTS WATCH WORLD REPORT 1993[8]
December, 1992
Iran is one of the worst violators of human rights in the Middle East. The government's response to unrest in mid-1992 led to greater abuse and repression. The reinvigorated campaign against "social vice" continues to restrict women, the media and the arts. Persecution of the Baha'is re-

mains a prominent feature of government policy. Assassinations and executions continue; opposition organizations are dismantled.

■ "[A]s economic unrest and discontent over high-handed government policies mounted, the rights climate worsened sharply."

■ "The summer of 1992 brought news of the stopping and arrest of many hundreds of women for violating *hejab* (mandatory veiling) in cities throughout Iran." Violations led to arrest, imprisonment, flogging or heavy fines.

■ Several more newspapers were banned in 1992.

■ There is "strict government control and censorship over the media."

■ Persecution of the Baha'is has "significantly abated" compared with the immediate post-revolutionary period. However, "Baha'is are not afforded official recognition, and enjoy no constitutional rights. They are denied the right to organize, profess or practice their religion. Discrimination in the form of restricted access to exit visas, university education, pensions, employment, public services and business licenses is commonplace."

■ Baha'i leader Bahman Samandari was summarily executed.

■ Persecution of evangelical Christians "showed no signs of abating in 1992."

■ The apparent execution of Ali Mohammad Kalantar, a member of the Iranian National Party, was a "disturbing sign that membership in non-violent opposition parties may also be deemed a capital offense."

■ "Monitoring of human rights conditions inside Iran is not permitted by the authorities."

AMNESTY INTERNATIONAL

Throughout 1992, Amnesty International reported on a number of human rights violations in Iran. Violations include political executions, unfair trials, assassinations and torture. No independent group in Iran is allowed to monitor or report human rights abuses and other measures of government repression.[9]

IRAN: EXECUTIONS OF PRISONERS CONTINUE UNABATED[10]

October 1, 1992

■ Most trials in Iran are secret and summary.

■ The second half of 1988 witnessed the most recent mass killing. At least 2,500 political prisoners were executed, including many "prisoners of conscience."

- In 1991, at least sixty Iranians were executed for "political activities."
- Some non-Islamic clergy have been murdered.
- The anti-drug campaign has resulted in hundreds of executions.

IRAN: UNFAIR TRIALS OF POLITICAL DETAINEES[11]
July, 1992
- According to reports Amnesty International "has received over the years, political trials are almost always held in secret, inside prisons, proceedings are summary, with no possibility for the detainee's family or even for defence counsel to attend."

IRAN: IMPRISONMENT, TORTURE, AND EXECUTION OF POLITICAL OPPONENTS[12]
January, 1992
- "Serious violations of human rights continued in the Islamic Republic of Iran during 1991, with hundreds of political arrests, unfair trials, torture and more than 750 executions."
- "There are no independent human rights or other concerned organizations in Iran to gather and assess human rights data, or assist those whose rights are violated to seek redress."
- The Iranian media is subject to "strict controls."
- Prisoners receive physical and psychological torture, including severe beatings on the soles of the feet.
- Allegations of extrajudicial execution of opposition activists abroad continue.

FREEDOM HOUSE
The Freedom House translates positions on major human rights issues into statistical rankings for political rights and civil liberties. The report incorporates information provided by the United Nations and other sources.

FREEDOM IN THE WORLD, POLITICAL RIGHTS & CIVIL LIBERTIES, 1991-1992[13]
Iran is categorized as "not free." On a scale of one to seven in which one represents the most free, Iran was rated a six on political rights and a five on civil liberties. Iranians are unable to democratically change their government, the media is state-controlled, execution and torture are common, women are victims of discrimination and freedom of association is strictly limited.

■ "A stringent religious test and the absence of organized, legal opposition prevents voters from having a free choice."

■ The state "represses" media attacks on the regime, Islam, Islamic government and the mistreatment of minorities.

■ In 1991, over 1,000 executions were announced.

■ "Officially-sanctioned physical and psychological torture is common in prison."

■ "Strict Islamic dress code for women is still strictly enforced."

■ "Non-Shiite religious groups face severe social and legal obstacles."

■ "Freedom of association is circumscribed. Private, independent organizations are rare."

POPULATION ACTION INTERNATIONAL

The most comprehensive statistical ranking is compiled by Population Action International. The report utilizes information provided by Freedom House and government sources.

THE INTERNATIONAL HUMAN SUFFERING INDEX (1992)[14]

One hundred forty-one countries were measured in ten areas of human welfare. The ratings ranged from 0, best, to 10, worst, in each category (Iran's scores are shown in parentheses): life expectancy (4), daily calorie supply (0), clean drinking water (2), infant immunization (3), secondary school enrollment (10), GNP per capita (7), rate of inflation (6), communications technology (8), political freedom (7) and civil rights (9). Most of the data is from official government sources, though the latter two categories are based on the Freedom House survey.

Iran's total score of 56 places it in the category of "high human suffering" (50-74 points) and seventy-second overall. Some neighboring scores: Afghanistan (89), Iraq (65), Pakistan (67) and Saudi Arabia (44).

U.S. OPERATIONAL POLICY TOWARD IRAN

U.S. policy toward Iran in 1994 is the result of over fourteen years of presidential and congressional action. A first wave of regulations paralleled the 1979-81 hostage crisis; this included a national emergency with respect to Iran, sundered diplomatic relations, the United States-Iran Claims Tribunal at The Hague and a travel advisory. While other regulations were put into effect at the time, these are the major ones that apply today.

In 1984, Secretary of State George Shultz designated Iran as a sponsor of international terrorism. U.S. antiterrorism law has evolved over the past few years, but it has consistently included several types of sanctions. This currently includes four major legislative acts with specific, automatic provisions for countries sponsoring terrorism. The Foreign Assistance Act bars several types of aid. The Arms Export Control Act prohibits transfers of many types of arms by the U.S. government or U.S. persons. The Export Administration Act restricts sales of goods and technology to Iran. The Foreign Operations, Export Financing and Related Programs Appropriations Act directs U.S. representatives to attempt to block international multilateral loans.

Two significant restrictions have been added since 1984, one by President Reagan and the other by Congress. In 1987, Reagan banned Iranian imports to the United States. In 1992, Congress passed the Iran-Iraq Arms Non-Proliferation Act which bars certain types of arms and technology transfers. The act includes sanctions against violators.

In a 1993 report, the U.S. Department of State summarized the significant barriers to U.S. exports to Iran: "[The] U.S. prohibits the export of items on the U.S. Munitions List, crime control and detection devices, chemical weapons precursors, nuclear and missile technology, and equipment used to manufacture military equipment. As a result of the Iran-Iraq Non-Proliferation Act...all goods exported to Iran which require a validated export license will be subject upon application to a policy of denial. This affects all dual-use commodities."[1] A U.S. Department of Commerce report explained that the act "mandates a strict policy of denial for applications to export dual-use items requiring a validated license to Iran."[2] Details of all these provisions and other minor ones follow.

NATIONAL EMERGENCY WITH RESPECT TO IRAN

The emergency was declared by President Jimmy Carter on November 14, 1979, in executive order 12170. It has been renewed annually by the president; the emergency automatically expires after one year unless it is renewed.[3]

Prepared by Jeremy Pressman

DIPLOMATIC RELATIONS

On April 7, 1980, President Carter broke diplomatic relations with Iran. They have not been restored. Pakistan represents Iranian interests in Washington. Switzerland represents U.S. interests in Teheran.[4]

UNITED STATES-IRAN CLAIMS TRIBUNAL AT THE HAGUE[5]

The tribunal was established as part of the January 1981 Algiers Accords ending the hostage crisis. President Carter announced the process on January 19, 1981. The tribunal first met in The Hague on July 1, 1981. The U.S. Department of the Treasury issued the Iranian Assets Control Regulations to facilitate the complex process of accounting for and dividing assets related to the Iran crisis.

The initial agreement set up three accounts to handle awards in disputes between Iran and the U.S. government, U.S. companies and U.S citizens. Dollar Account No. 1 began with $3.7 billion and was to be used for claims of bank syndicates that included a U.S. bank. Dollar Account No. 2 began with $1.4 billion and was to be used for nonsyndicated U.S. bank claims. The Security Account, for awards to U.S. nationals and the U.S. government, began with $1 billion; Iran must replenish it whenever it falls below $500 million. However, as of September 28, 1993, the Security Account stood at only $214 million.

The Iranian Foreign Military Sales program was a fourth area not covered by these accounts. In 1979, the program included over 2,800 contracts and $20 billion. Payment for each contract was made to a trust fund and reduced as the contracts were carried out. After the revolution, Iran laid claim to the balance in the trust fund and asked for compensation for the military equipment purchased but not exported. President Bush reported on November 29, 1990, that "in return for Iran's agreement not to seek return of the full balance of its Foreign Military Sales Trust Fund from the United States in advance of adjudication of its claims on the merits, the United States transferred $200 million from the Trust Fund to the Security Account..."

In November 1991 Iran and the United States agreed on $278 million as compensation for undelivered Iranian-owned, American-made military equipment from the prerevolutionary period. The sum of $260 million was paid directly to Iran while the remaining $18 million was added to the Security Account. Other Iranian claims in the military field are close to $10 billion, though a former State Department legal adviser, Abraham Sofaer, estimates that the actual amount owed is closer to $1 billion.

As of October 1, 1993, the tribunal had rendered a total of 547 awards.

More than 85 percent of large claims (more than $250,000) by U.S. nationals have been adjudicated, settled or withdrawn.

On May 13, 1990, Iran and the United States settled all small claims. The United States was awarded $105 million from the Security Account, of which $50 million was set aside to pay small claims. The Foreign Claims Settlement Commission at the Department of Justice was charged with hearing the claims and has, as of October 1, 1993, issued decisions for 1,568 of the 3,112 small claims.

Cases between the Iranian Bank Markazi and U.S. bank syndicates have been almost completely resolved. Dollar Account No. 1 was closed in 1992. Most of these funds had gone to repay of syndicated bank loans in 1981. Most nonsyndicated U.S. bank claims were resolved by 1986. The tribunal has also dealt with dual national claims.

SPONSORSHIP OF INTERNATIONAL TERRORISM

On January 13, 1984, Secretary of State George Shultz designated Iran as a supporter of international terrorism.[6] As a result, the following measures are currently in effect.

Foreign Assistance Act[7]

Section 620(a) of the Foreign Assistance Act stipulates that the United States cannot provide any assistance under the Foreign Assistance Act, the Agricultural Trade Development and Assistance Act of 1954, the Peace Corps Act, or the Export-Import Bank Act of 1945 to any country if "the Secretary of State determines that the government of that country has repeatedly provided support for acts of international terrorism." Section 620(d) gives the president limited waiver authority if justified by "national security interests or humanitarian reasons."

Arms Export Control Act[8]

Section 38(a)(2) of the Arms Export Control Act requires that decisions on issuing export licenses under section 38 take into account whether the export of an article will support international terrorism. Section 40(a) prohibits the United States Government from exporting or otherwise providing (including by sale, lease, loan or grant), directly or indirectly, any item enumerated on the United States Munitions List. Targeted countries are also prohibited from acquiring "any munitions item" with U.S. credits, guarantees or other financial assistance under the authority of the Arms Export Control Act, the Foreign Assistance Act of 1961, or any other law.

The same section continues by precluding U.S. government consent to the transfer of any munitions item and the granting of an export license "for any export or transfer (including by means of a technical assistance agreement, manufacturing licensing agreement, or coproduction agreement)." Prohibited transactions by United States persons are similar to above. These prohibitions apply to "a country if the Secretary of State determines that the government of that country has repeatedly provided support for acts of international terrorism." The president has waiver authority with respect to a specific transaction if justified by "national security interests."

Export Administration Act of 1979[9]

In the Export Administration Act, section 6(j) requires a "validated license...for the export of goods or technology to a country" if the secretary of state has determined that the government of such country has repeatedly provided support for acts on international terrorism or the export of such goods or technology "could make a significant contribution to the military potential of such country, including its military logistics capability, or could enhance the ability of such country to support acts of international terrorism." Section 6(l) explains that licenses for the export of missile technology will be denied "if the ultimate consignee of the goods or technology is a facility in a country the government of which has been determined under subsection (j) to have repeatedly provided support for acts of international terrorism."

Foreign Operations, Export Financing and Related Programs Appropriations Act, 1991[10]

According to section 555, the secretary of the treasury instructs the United States executive director of each international financial institution "to vote against any loan or other use of funds of the respective institution to or for a country" for which the secretary of state has determined that the country supports international terrorism, as explained in the Export Administration Act of 1979. This includes the International Bank for Reconstruction and Development, the International Development Association, the International Monetary Fund, the Inter-American Development Bank, the Asian Development Bank, the African Development Bank, and the African Development Fund.

The export controls were expanded by President Reagan on September 27, 1984; September 25, 1987; and October 26, 1987. Under the authority of the 1979 Export Administration Act, controls were imposed on Iran restricting, among other items, sales of aircraft, helicopters, related parts and components, chemical weapons precursors, crime control items, all goods and technical data destined to a military end-user or end-use, SCUBA gear and related diving equipment, mobile communications equipment, boats (including inflatable boats), off-highway wheel tractors, large diesel engines, nonstrategic aircraft parts and components, portable electric generators, marine engines, other naval equipment, underwater photographic equipment, submersible systems, pressured aircraft breathing equipment, sonar navigation equipment, electronic test equipment and cryptographic equipment.[11]

BAN ON IRANIAN IMPORTS

On October 6, 1987, Congress passed resolutions calling for the prohibition of Iranian imports. The Senate resolution (S.R. 1748) passed unanimously while the House version (H.R. 3391) was approved 407 to 5. Further congressional action was preempted by the president. On October 29, 1987, President Reagan issued executive order 12613 banning nearly all imports from Iran. Only news material, petroleum products refined from Iranian oil by a third party, and Iranian-origin goods located outside of Iran before the embargo was imposed (mostly "nonfungible" goods like carpets) were exempted. President Reagan said he was responding to Iranian-sponsored terrorism and attacks on Persian Gulf shipping.

Reagan's executive order was further defined in the November 17, 1987, Iranian Transactions Regulations issued by the secretary of the treasury. These set forth detailed licensing procedures for goods exempted from the import ban and exempted a fourth category of goods, those related to awards at the United States-Iran Claims Tribunal.

Amendments were made in 1991 allowing the import of Iranian oil if the proceeds were solely used to replenish Iranian funds for tribunal payments; tightened documentation requirements for carpets; and eased controls on household items and personal effects.[12]

IRAN-IRAQ ARMS NON-PROLIFERATION ACT OF 1992[13]

The Iran-Iraq Arms Non-Proliferation Act was passed as Title 16 of the National Defense Authorization Act for fiscal year 1993 (H.R. 5006). The general goal of the act is to oppose any transfer that aids Iranian or Iraqi attempts to acquire "chemical, biological, nuclear, or destabilizing numbers and types of advanced conventional weapons." The sanctions against Iran are taken from the Iraq Sanctions Act of 1990. Foreign Military

Sales are banned; no licenses may be issued for items on the U.S. Munitions List and certain goods and technologies on control lists of the Export Administration Act of 1979 are prohibited. Lastly, in the nuclear field, section 1603 blocks NRC and Department of Energy licenses as well as the distribution of any nuclear material.

Section 1604 bars the U.S. government from entering into contracts with any person (or legal entity) violating the sanctions against Iran or Iraq and denies them export licenses for two years. Section 1605 dictates mandatory sanctions against any foreign government that contributes to the advanced conventional weaponry of Iran or Iraq. These one-year sanctions include the suspension of U.S. assistance and codevelopment or coproduction agreements, opposition to multilateral development bank assistance, suspension of military and dual-use technical exchange agreements and a ban on the export of items from the U.S. Munitions List.

The president may waive sections 1603 to 1605 if "essential to the national interest of the United States." The original Senate version, sponsored by Sen. John McCain, would have eliminated this discretionary waiver authority. It would still have allowed the waiver of sanctions against persons or foreign governments, however.

In 1993, Senator McCain and Sen. Joseph Lieberman introduced the Iran-Iraq Arms Non-Proliferation Amendments of 1993 (S.1172). These would expand and toughen numerous aspects of the current law. Major amendments would increase the number of mandatory and discretionary sanctions against persons helping Iran or Iraq, raise the number of discretionary sanctions against foreign countries aiding Iran or Iraq, allow the president to modify (rather than simply waive) sanctions and add definitions of more key terms. This last addition includes weapons of mass destruction, a broad definition that covers bombers with ranges of more than 600 nautical miles and missiles.

ADDITIONAL CONGRESSIONAL ACTION AGAINST IRAN

As in past years, the Foreign Operations, Export Financing, and Related Programs Appropriations Act for fiscal year 1993, passed on October 6, 1992, bars the use of funds to directly or indirectly finance any assistance or reparations to Iran and several other countries. The foreign operations bill for fiscal year 1994 reduced the Clinton administration's request for paid-in capital to the World Bank by $14 million "to protest approximately $477 in World Bank loans to Iran."[14]

Congress has also regularly asked the president to focus international attention on the plight of the Baha'i community in Iran. A resolution passed in summer 1992 calls human rights and especially the treatment of the Baha'i "a significant element in the development of U.S.-Iranian relations." Similar resolutions have been proposed in 1993.

A number of bills introduced during the 102nd Congress would have imposed other interesting restrictions. Rep. Charles Schumer's bill would have prohibited arms transfers to certain countries (Iran, Iraq, Jordan, Kuwait, Saudi Arabia, Libya, Syria, Qatar, Bahrain, Yemen, Lebanon, Oman, UAE) unless they end their state of war with Israel and accord formal recognition to the sovereignty of Israel. Rep. Sam Gejdenson proposed a three-year ban on exports of controlled goods or technology and defense articles or services to Iran, Iraq, Syria, and Libya because these countries sponsor terrorism. Rep. Jon Kyl proposed that the United States block increases in its IMF quota if Russia, among other things, transfers Kilo-class submarines to Iran or trains a crew for the submarines.[15]

RESTRICTED TRAVEL TO IRAN

On January 27, 1981, the State Department issued a statement superseding the April 1980 ban on travel to Iran. In the new statement, "the Department of State strongly urges United States citizens to avoid any travel to Iran." In a Consular Information Sheet dated August 31, 1993, the State Department warned "all U.S. citizens against travel to Iran, where danger continues to exist because of the generally anti-American atmosphere and Iranian government hostility to the U.S. government."[16]

SHIPPING

In an executive branch policy reiterated in 1991, Iranian ships are barred from U.S. ports.[17]

PISTACHIO TARIFF

A countervailing duty on Iranian pistachios was imposed in late 1986 after U.S. growers pursued unfair trade actions on the basis of dumping and government subsidies. ("The unfair trade actions, in effect, resulted in a tariff of 283% ad valorem for raw and 317.89% for roasted pistachios.") The duty, which has never been rescinded, was superseded by the October 1987 embargo on Iranian imports. Some U.S. growers cited Iranian hostility toward the United States as one justification for the trade action. In late 1991, the Department of Commerce began an administrative review of the countervailing duty, but the review was discontinued in 1992 under pressure from U.S. growers.[18]

END NOTES

INTRODUCTION

[1] In a radio speech the day before Khamenei said, "The United States is the dictatorship which the Muslim nation drove from its home with empty hands and there is no need whatsoever for us to negotiate with dictators." He also called those Iranians seeking a dialogue with the United States "simple-minded, fearful and politically naive." Chris Hedges, "Iranians, Marking '79 Crisis, Assail U.S. as Rift Again Widens," *New York Times*, November 5, 1993.

[2] "Clinton Called the Most Hated by Muslims for Rushdie Visit," *New York Times*, November 27, 1993, p. 5.

[3] Interview on *Larry King Live*, June 28, 1993, transcribed in Federal News Service, #CK-28-06-E, p. 2.

[4] Kenneth Katzman, "Iran: Current Developments and U.S. Policy," Congressional Research Service Issue Brief 93033, February 11, 1993, p. 13; see also A. M. Rosenthal, "The U.S.-Iran Oil Scam," *New York Times*, July, 16, 1993, p. A15.

U.S. POLICY AND THE IRANIAN CHALLENGE

[1] Steve Coll, "Technology from West Floods Iran," *Washington Post*, November 10, 1992, pp. A1, A28. Like the 1993 CRS report mentioned earlier, the *Post* uses the $3.5 billion figure for purchases of Iranian oil by U.S. companies. For details on rebuilding and American oil purchases, see James Tanner, "Back in Business: Iran's Oil Production Is Soaring, with Help from American Firms," *Wall Street Journal*, November 25, 1992, pp. A1, A9.

[2] Regulations pertaining to the Iran-Iraq Arms Non-Proliferation Act of October 1992 block the export of navigation, direction finding and radar equipment; certain digital computers; and some software. For further information on the act, see Appendix IV. The Commerce Department itself has argued that this act has tightened the control of U.S. dual use exports to Iran (Katzman, "Iran: Current Developments," p. 12). A general State Department breakdown of U.S. exports to Iran does not list any of the above-mentioned items, though the nature of hundreds of millions of dollars worth of 1992 and 1993 (through June) exports is not specified. The list of items for export to Iran subject on application to a policy of denial

and the trade breakdown are available through the U.S. Department of State's Flashfax system (202-482-1064). "Statistics on U.S.-Iranian Trade," exact date in second half of 1993 unclear due to poor transmission, table 8, no. 0500, p. 14; and "Trade with Iran," December 1992, no. 0501, pp. 1-2.

[3] Excerpts from Martin Indyk's on-the-record address delivered May 18, 1993 at the Washington Institute for Near East Policy. Martin Indyk, "Clinton Administration Policy Toward the Middle East," *Policy Watch*, no. 84, Washington Institute for Near East Policy, May 21, 1993, p. 3. That the international media has latched onto the confrontational aspects of the "dual containment" policy and ignored its more substantive and less strident components is typical of the dilemma policymakers face when seeking a succinct phrase to describe a new policy only to have it backfire. In April 1981, in preparation for his first visit to the Middle East as secretary of state, Alexander Haig was asked at a press gathering what he hoped to achieve on the trip. The phrase that emerged was "strategic consensus." What Haig meant was to focus on the common interests of the United States, its conservative Arab friends and Israel, in facing up to the regional threats posed by the Soviet Union and its surrogates. While privately all the key Arab leaders Haig talked to (President Sadat, King Hussein and King Khalid) agreed with him, they could not say so in public and had to revert to their standard rhetoric that the Palestinian problem was the most dangerous threat to the region. Haig was consequently credited with a failure to achieve "strategic consensus."

[4] See R. Jeffrey Smith and Daniel Williams, "White House to Step Up Plans to Isolate Iran, Iraq," *Washington Post*, May 23, 1993, p. A26; Douglas Jehl, "Fearing More Hostility from Iran, U.S. Considers Move to Isolate It," *New York Times*, May 27, 1993, p. A1.

[5] John Goshko, "U.S. Urges Halt to Iran Sales," *Washington Post*, June 10, 1993, p. A27

[6] See testimony of Edward Djerejian, Assistant Secretary for Near Eastern and South Asian Affairs, before the Subcommittee on Europe and the Middle East of the House Foreign Affairs Committee, "Developments in the Middle East," July 27, 1993.

[7] Anthony Lake, "Confronting Backlash States," *Foreign Affairs*, vol. 73, no. 2, March/April, 1994, pp. 45-55.

[8] Some examples of recent writings that call for a more conciliatory approach to Iran are Shireen Hunter, "Iran through a Distorted Lens," *Christian Science Monitor*, March 2, 1992, p. 4; commentary from *al-Majalla* in "Saudi Editor Predicts a Brave New Iran," *Mideast Mirror*, June 18, 1993, pp. 20-21; R. K. Ramazani, "Iran's Foreign Policy: Both North and South," *Middle East Journal*, Summer 1992, pp. 393-412; Amin Saikal, "The United States and Persian Gulf Security," *World Policy Journal*, Summer, 1992, pp. 515-31; and James A. Bill, "Iran: The Prodigal Returns," *World Monitor*, March 1989, pp. 64-71.

The most consistent pro-regime publication in the U.S. is the *U.S.-Iran Review*, a newsletter published by the Forum on American-Iranian Relations (FAIR). The newsletter articulates a positive and nonthreatening view of Iran. FAIR bolsters the image and credentials of Iran, often with the writings of respected U.S. scholars; however the newsletter and FAIR policy papers rarely contain pieces critical of the Islamic regime. Iran's opposition to the Arab-Israeli peace process and the Israel-PLO agreement is dismissed as mere rhetoric. It has called Western support for the Arab position on Abu Musa an attempt "to set up a straw claim to justify a possible future military action against Iran." The results of Rafsanjani's 1993 re-election bid, in which his share of the vote fell by more than 30 percent and voter turnout dropped 14 percent, it sees neither as troubling for the Islamic regime nor significantly different from past outcomes. In interpreting the Iranian buildup, one policy paper warned U.S. officials "not to succumb to an ideologically-based and fear-mongering industry which is emerging...to justify institutions whose existence depends on creating another American enemy." The same paper calls on observers "to focus on Iran's military capabilities rather than on its perceived intentions." A summary of recent conferences noted that participants deplored "Iran's *alleged* political assassinations" (emphasis added).

Such an approach toward Iran leads to a conciliatory U.S. policy prescription. FAIR's plan of April 1993 proposes five steps to jump start a dialogue: both sides should deflate their "super-charged rhetoric"; the United States should release Iranian assets, end the ban on Iranian imports and pursue opportunities for cooperation (such as encouraging the international community to provide humanitarian refugee aid). The only task the plan assigns to Iran is to clarify policy intentions by designating official government spokesmen.

The FAIR Foundation describes itself as "a private, nonpartisan and nonprofit organization whose purpose is to promote a dialogue for better understanding between American and Iranian people." The November

1993 issue of *U.S.-Iran Review* (vol.1, no. 8), states that the "FAIR Foundation does not accept contributions by any government." According to U.S. Department of Justice documents the FAIR Foundation was registered with the Justice Department for a one month period (July 30, 1992 to August 27, 1992) and the government of Iran was to provide seed money to start up the Foundation.

[9] Hard line articles about Iran include Jack Anderson and Michael Binstein, "Iran's Still-Elusive Moderates," *Washington Post*, April 18, 1993; David Hoffman, "Israel Seeking to Convince U.S. That West Is Threatened by Iran," *Washington Post*, March 13, 1993; Michael Collins Dunn, "More Questions about Iran's Intentions in the Gulf," *The Washington Report on Middle East Affairs*, July 1992, p. 31; Michael Collins Dunn, "Iran's Alarming Military Buildup Transfixes Wary Gulf Neighbors," *The Washington Report on Middle East Affairs*, October, 1992, p. 35; Israel Shahak, "With Iraq Neutralized, Israelis Seek Catalysts for War with Iran," *The Washington Report on Middle East Affairs*, April/May, 1993, pp. 15-16; James Woolsey (CIA Director) "Iran Is the Most Active and Dangerous Sponsor of Terrorism," *Mideast Mirror*, April 22, 1993, pp. 16-17; Ian Alexander, "Troubled Oil," *National Review*, August 9, 1993, pp. 45-47; "Iran: A Threat to World Peace," *New India-Times*, July 23, 1993, p. 55; Aluf Ben, "A New Enemy in the Region," *Ha'aretz* (Israel), March 4, 1993, in FBIS-NES, March 5, 1993, pp. 28-29; Tom Masland, "The Threat That Gets Overlooked: Iran," *Newsweek*, January 25, 1993, p. 43; Charles Krauthammer, "Iran: Orchestrator of Disorder," *Washington Post*, January 1, 1993, p. 19; and Amos Perlmutter, "Before Iran Gets the Bomb," *Washington Times*, November 23, 1993, p. A15.

The People's Mojahedin is the primary Iranian opposition group in the United States and a relentless advocate of continued hostility toward the Iranian government. It seeks the violent overthrow of the Iranian regime. Regular reports and press releases condemn the Iranian government and challenge international supporters of the regime. *Islamic Fundamentalism: The New Global Threat*, a Mojahedin book by Mohammad Mohaddessin, director of international relations, details the "octopus" of the Iranian fundamentalist government; it contends that the "long arm of Iran's terrorists" reaches to South Asia, Argentina, Europe and across the Middle East. The book asserts that Islamic fundamentalism is based on "medieval and totalitarian ideology" and, "owing to its nature, this ideology...elevates the export of revolution, crisis, and disruption of all norms of international relations to the top of its agenda." The book is filled with absolutist statements about the ideology and policies of the Iranian government.

Yet Mojahedin claims do reach the Western media. The People's Mojahedin is often cited by Rowland Evans and Robert Novak, who call the group the "key anti-fundamentalist resistance." (For example, see Evans and Novak, "Iran's New Satellite", *Washington Post*, August 19, 1993, p. A29; or Evans and Novak, "Russian Tanks in Tehran," *Washington Post*, February 5, 1992.) In Congress, some representatives have called for an official dialogue with the Mojahedin and also rely on Mojahedin intelligence about Iran. Critics, however, remain wary of the Mojahedin; its National Liberation Army is based in Iraq and has received support from Saddam Hussein's government. Some opponents, including the U.S. Department of State, cite connections to the murder of Americans in Iran in the 1970s. Others allege past Marxist leanings.

[10] For an interesting and cogent presentation of this line of argument, see Patrick Clawson, *Iran's Challenge to the West: How, When and Why* (Washington, D.C.: Washington Institute for Near East Policy, 1993), pp. 37-42.

[11] Zbigniew Brzezinski, *Out of Control: Global Turmoil on the Eve of the Twenty-First Century* (New York: Scribner, 1993), p. 162.

THE ROOTS OF AMERICAN-IRANIAN ENMITY

[1] T. H. Vail Motter, *United States Army in World War II, The Middle East Theater: The Persian Corridor and Aid to Russia* (Washington, D.C.: Office of the Chief of Military History, Department of the Army, 1952).

[2] Richard F. Nyrop, editor, *Iran: A Country Study* (Washington, D.C.: The American University, 1978), pp. 58-62.

[3] Robert Mantel and Geoffrey Kemp, *U.S. Military Sales to Iran*, Staff Report to the Subcommittee on Foreign Assistance, U.S. Senate (Washington, D.C.: U.S. Government Printing Office, 1976).

[4] For details of the Carter administration's agonies over Iran, see Gary Sick, *All Fall Down: America's Tragic Encounter with Iran* (New York: Random House, 1985).

⁵ The G-7 (Group of Seven) nations are Canada, France, Germany, Italy, Japan, the United Kingdom and the United States.

⁶ John M. Goshko, "U.S. Urges Halt to Iran Sales," *Washington Post*, June 10, 1993, p. A27.

⁷ Robert S. Greenberger, "Iran's Economic Problems Could Spark Friction Between U.S. and Its Allies," *Wall Street Journal*, January 3, 1994, p.8.

IRAN'S DOMESTIC PROBLEMS

¹ Good background reading on recent Iranian political and economic developments can be found in: Jahangir Amuzegar, *Iran's Economy under the Islamic Republic* (New York: St. Martin's Press, forthcoming); Shaul Bakhash, *The Reign of the Ayatollahs: Iran and the Islamic Revolution* (New York: Basic Books, 1984); Shahram Chubin and Charles Tripp, *Iran and Iraq at War* (Boulder, Colo.: Westview Press, 1988); Shireen Hunter, *Iran after Khomenei* (Westport, Conn.: Greenwood Publishing Group, 1992); Robin Wright, *In the Name of God: The Khomenei Decade* (New York: Simon and Schuster, 1989); Graham E. Fuller, *The Center of the Universe: The Geopolitics of Iran* (Boulder, Colo.: Westview Press, 1991); R. K. Ramazani, *Revolutionary Iran: Challenge and Response in the Middle East* (Baltimore: Johns Hopkins University Press, 1988).

² Jahangir Amuzegar, "The Iranian Economy before and after the Revolution," *Middle East Journal*, Summer, 1992, pp. 413-25; Clawson, *Iran's Challenge to the West*; for more detailed information, see Organisation for Economic Cooperation and Development, *External Debt Statistics* (Paris: OECD, 1992); and International Monetary Fund, *International Financial Statistics Yearbook* (Washington, D.C.: IMF, 1992).

³ Katzman, "Iran: Current Developments," p. 5.

⁴ The contentious issue of monetary donations to the Iranian clergy was discussed in a speech by Ayatollah Ahmad Jannati at Teheran University. *Voice of the Islamic Republic of Iran*, August 14, 1992 in FBIS-NES, August 18, 1992, p.42.

⁵ See Chris Hedges, "Rafsanjani Re-elected in Iran, But Without a Huge Mandate," *New York Times*, June 14, 1993, p. A8; and Nora Boustany,

"Iranian Reelected Amid Signs of Discontent," *Washington Post*, June 14, 1993, p. A20.

[6] See "Reform-Minded Finance Minister Is Rejected by Iranian Parliament," *New York Times*, August 17, 1993, p. A10; and Safa Haeri, "Humiliation for Rafsanjani," *MEI*, August 28, 1993, p. 13.

[7] Private communication with Dr. Abdel Monem Said Aly in Salzburg, Austria in July 1993. Also see Shahram Chubin, *Iran's National Security Policy: Intentions, Capabilities and Impact* (Washington, D.C.: Carnegie Endowment for International Peace, forthcoming 1994), and Clawson, *Iran's Challenge to the West*, p. 41.

IRAN AND ITS NEIGHBORS

[1] See Clawson, *Iran's Challenge to the West*, pp. 72 -75.

[2] For an interesting review by a young Russian scholar of Russian arms sales, see Andrei Volpin, "Russian Arms Sales Policy Toward the Middle East," Research Memorandum #2B (Washington, D.C.: The Washington Institute for Near East Policy) 1993.

[3] Interfax, March 31, 1993 in FBIS-SOV, March 31, 1993, p. 8-9.

[4] See John P. Hannah, "'The Last Thrust Southward': Zhirinovsky and the Middle East," *Policywatch*, no. 108, Washington Institute for Near East Policy, December 28, 1993.

[5] The Economic Cooperation Council (ECO), reactivated in 1985 under its present name, was formerly known as the Regional Cooperation for Development (established in 1965 by Iran, Pakistan and Turkey). The organization, which had little impact until 1992, assumed greater significance as a potential vehicle for regional economic cooperation that would include the new Central Asian republics after the breakup of the former Soviet Union. Expansion in its membership was approved at a heads of state summit in 1992, and the ECO now consists of Afganistan, Azerbaijan, Iran, Kazakhstan, Kyrgyzstan, Pakistan, Tajikistan, Turkey, Turkmenistan and Uzbekistan. Turkey would also like the Turkish Republic of Northern Cyprus to be an associate member.

The ECO is headquartered in Teheran and its declared purpose is to promote regional cooperation in trade, transportation, communications, tourism, cultural affairs and economic development. The future course and effectiveness of ECO remains in doubt because of the conflict for leadership between Iran, which views it as a means for establishing a future Islamic common market to promote Islamic values, and Turkey, which insists that it remains a strictly secular body to promote free trade and develop the region's infrastructure. Arthur S. Banks, ed., *Political Handbook of the World 1992* (New York: CSA Publications, 1992), p. 922.

[6] Islamic Republic News Agency (IRNA), October 27, 1992 in FBIS-NES, October 28, 1992, pp. 48-49.

[7] Besides bilateral agreements, Turkey and Iran have both concluded regional cooperation agreements with the Central Asian republics. In February 1992, Turkey formed the Black Sea Economic Cooperation Zone, which included Russia, Azerbaijan and the five Central Asian states. Iran has formed the Caspian Sea Organization, which includes Kazakhstan, Turkmenistan, Russia and Azerbaijan.

[8] "Mumcu Laid to Rest," *Turkish Daily News*, January 28, 1993, p. 8.

[9] "Turkey Asserts Islamic Ring That Killed Three Has Iran Links," *New York Times*, February 5, 1993, p. A6.

[10] Alan Cowell, "Turkey's Fight against Kurds Embarrasses Allies," *New York Times*, September 7, 1992, p. A3.

[11] James Dorsey, "Armenia to Sign Accord with Iran for Natural Gas," *Washington Times*, April 2, 1993, p. A10; for information on oil talks, see *2000 Ikibin'e Dogru* (Turkey), October 4, 1992 in FBIS-SOV, October 15, 1992, p. 51.

[12] "Energy Crisis Forces Armenia to Regional Solutions," *Turkish Daily News*, December 11, 1992, pp. 1, 11.

[13] Dorsey, "Armenia to Sign Accord."

[14] "Caucasus City Falls to Armenian Forces," *New York Times*, August 24, 1993, p. A7. An unofficial translation of the August 12 statement was released by the press section of the permanent mission to the United Nations of the Islamic Republic of Iran, "Foreign Ministry Statement of 12

August 93 on Armenian Operations in Fuzuli (Azarbaijan [sic])," no. 088, August 16, 1993. Armenians actually view relations as improving and see such Iranian declarations as irrelevant. Felix Corley, "Balancing Act," *MEI*, no. 457, August 28, 1993, p. 15.

[15] *Al-Sharq Al-Awsat*, February 25-26, 1993 in FBIS-NES, March 4, 1993, p. 52.

[16] Firuz Kazemzadeh, testimony before the Helsinki Commission (U.S.), March 25, 1993.

[17] Interview by author with senior specialists for Central Asia in Russian Foreign Ministry, May 1993.

[18] For information on Islamic friendship and building stronger ties, see PTV Television Network (Pakistan), August 28, 1993 in FBIS-NES, August 31, 1993, pp. 56-57; IRNA, March 22, 1993, from Middle East News Network, March 25, 1993; and an article on Iranian President Rafsanjani's visit to Pakistan in *Deutsche Press-Agentur*, September 8, 1992. For an article on the Economic Cooperation Organization, see *Jahan-e Eslam*, February 14, 1993, from Middle East News Network, February 26, 1993. For articles on Iran and Pakistan in Afghanistan, see IRIB Television, March 6, 1993 from Middle East News Network, March 9, 1993; *Ettela'at*, February 9, 1993, from Middle East News Network, February 26, 1993; and, for a review of strains caused by Afghanistan, *Interpress*, August 1, 1992. For Indian fears, see Raju Gopalakrishnan, "Pak-Iran Unholy Alliance Against India," *News India*, April 16, 1993, p. 12. Rumors that Iran agreed to underwrite the Pakistani defense budget in exchange for nuclear technology are contained in *The Nation*, April 15, 1993, from Middle East News Network, April 20, 1993.

[19] "Indian Defence Ministry Terms Iran a 'Security Threat,' " *These Days*, April 14, 1993, p. 3.

[20] "Close Ties with Iran Mooted," *Times of India*, September 21, 1993.

[21] "Better Indo-Iranian Ties," *Indian Express*, September 24, 1993; "Path-breaking Visit," *The Economic Times*, September 24, 1993; and "Turning Point in Indo-Iranian Ties," *The Independent* (India), exact date unknown.

22 The most recent Abu Musa conflict began in March 1992, when Iranian forces expelled all foreigners, including United Arab Emirates citizens who provided essential services for the UAE government. These included teachers, engineers in charge of water facilities and health workers. Previously, Iran and Sharjah, one of the seven emirates of the UAE, had jointly governed the island under a 1971 agreement. Iran claims it took the measures because of security concerns about the island. The UAE contends the Iranian government is expansionist. The crisis reached its peak on August 24, 1992, when Iranian officials prevented one hundred residents, including UAE citizens, from landing on the island. See "Gulf States Fear Iran Is the New Bully," *Toronto Star*, September 29, 1992, p. 2; Youssef Ibrahim, "Dispute over Gulf Islands Worsens Iran-Arab Ties," *New York Times*, October 4, 1992, p. 11.

23 "Comfort Blanket for the Gulf," *The Economist*, December 5, 1992, pp. 39-40.

24 The GCC issued the Abu Dhabi Declaration on December 23, 1992. Amidst a general spirit of cooperation and unity at the 13th GCC summit, the text rejected the acquisition of territory by force and emphasized UAE sovereignty over Abu Musa and the Tunb Islands. In addition to calling for the continued development of GCC defense and security capabilities, the declaration contained references to Somalia, Bosnia and the Palestinians. For the declaration, see WAKH, December 23, 1992 in FBIS-NES, December 24, 1992, p.1.

25 IRIB Television First Program, December 23, 1992 in FBIS-NES, December 28, 1992, p. 55.

26 Agence France Presse, Paris, April 5, 1993, in FBIS-NES, April 6, 1993, p. 16.

27 A good overview of the emerging security problems of the Arab Gulf states can be found in Joseph A. Kechichian, *Political Dynamics and Security in the Arabian Peninsula Through the 1990s* (Santa Monica, California: RAND, 1993).

28 R. K. Ramazani, "Iran's Foreign Policy: Both North and South," *Middle East Journal*, 46, no. 3, (Summer 1992) p. 399.

[29] *Vision of the Islamic Republic of Iran*, January 4, 1993, in FBIS-NES, January 6, 1993, p. 58.

[30] James Tanner and Bhushan Bahree, "Iran Is Increasing Oil Output to Use as Bargaining Chip at OPEC Meeting," *Wall Street Journal*, September 8, 1992, p. A9.

[31] Ramazani, "Iran's Foreign Policy," p. 400.

[32] Agence France Presse, September 25, 1992, in FBIS-NES, September 25, 1992, p. 10.

[33] Agence France Presse, November 3, 1992, in FBIS-NES, November 6, 1992, pp. 17-18.

[34] Agence France Presse, February 6, 1993, in FBIS-NES, February 8, 1993, p. 29.

[35] Ramazani, "Iran's Foreign Policy," p. 401.

[36] IRNA, February 16, 1993, in FBIS-NES, February 17, 1993, p. 13.

[37] Ramazani, "Iran's Foreign Policy," p. 401.

[38] *Misr Al-Fatah*, October 12, 1992, in FBIS-NES, October 16, 1992, p. 13.

[39] *Al-Hayah*, January 24, 1993, in FBIS-NES, January 28, 1993, p. 15.

[40] Ibid., p. 16.

HOW DANGEROUS IS IRAN?

[1] See Shahram Chubin, *Iran's National Security Policy: Intentions, Capabilities and Impact* (Washington, D.C.: Carnegie Endowment for International Peace, forthcoming 1994).

[2] Testimony of Robert Gates, director of the Central Intelligence Agency, before the Defense Policy Panel and the Department of Energy Defense Nuclear Facilities Panel of the House Armed Services Commit-

tee, "Regional Threats and Defense Options for the 1990s" March 27, 1992, H.A.S.C. no. 102-73, p. 317.

[3] Islamic Republic of Iran Permanent Mission to the United Nations, "Defence Minister: Iran Will Not Be Dragged Into Mid East Arms Race," release no. 075, April 15, 1993.

[4] Chubin, *Iran's National Security Policy*. See also Anthony Cordesman, "Iran and Iraq: The Military Dimension of Possible Regional Conflict," paper prepared for meeting of the American Association for the Advancement of Science, Barcelona, Spain, October 1993; W. Seth Carus, "Proliferation and Security in South West Asia," paper prepared for 1993 U.S. Central Command South West Asia Symposium, May 1993; Henry Sokolski, "Iran: Willing to War, Still Wanting the Way," paper prepared for Center for Strategic and International Studies Regional Dynamics and Global Weapons Proliferation Project, November 9, 1993.

[5] Chubin, *Iran's National Security Policy*.

[6] "Lo-lo-lo" means the aircraft flies to and from the target at low altitudes which causes it to consume a great deal of fuel. "Hi-lo-hi" means flying to and from the aircraft at high altitudes and only flying low when delivering its weapons load over the target. *The Military Balance: 1988-1989* (London: International Institute for Strategic Studies, 1989), pp. 240-41.

[7] *The Military Balance: 1993-1994* (London: The International Institute for Strategic Studies, 1993), pp. 111, 115-16; and "Iran Cancels Russian Deals," *Middle East Defense News*, March 1, 1993, p. 4.

[8] Glen Howard, "Rebuilding the Iranian Air Force," *FSRC Analytical Note*, December 10, 1992, p. 3.

[9] See Sokolski, "Iran: Willing to War," p. 34.

[10] Ibid., p. 2.

[11] "Iran/Russia Wrap up $2 Billion Arms Deal," *Flight International*, July 21, 1992, p. 13.

[12] Youssef Ibrahim, "Iran Said to Commit $7 Billion to Secret Arms Plan," *New York Times*, August 8, 1992, p. 3.

[13] "Iran Cancels," *Middle East Defense News*, p. 5.

[14] Missile ranges and payloads may vary slightly due to local modifications. "The Proliferation of Ballistic Missiles," *Arms Control Today*, April 1992, p. 29; Joseph Bermudez, "Ballistic Ambitions Ascendant," *Jane's Defence Weekly*, April 10, 1993, p. 22.

[15] Knut Royce, "Iran Buying 150 'Terror' Missiles," *Long Island Newsday*, April 11, 1992, p. 6.

[16] Royce, "150 Terror Missiles"; see also Douglas Jehl, "Iran Is Reported Acquiring Missiles," *New York Times*, April 8, 1993, p. A9.

[17] Alan George, "Libya Sells Al Fatah Design to Iranians," *Flight International*, April 20, 1993, p. 4.

[18] Christopher Walker, "Iran's Submarine Purchase Tilts Gulf Power Balance," *The London Times*, October 5, 1992, p. 9.

[19] Joris Janssen Lok, "Russia Delivers First 'Kilo' to Iran," *Jane's Defence Weekly*, November 21, 1992, p. 9.

[20] "Iran Receives Russian Sub," *Radio Free Europe/Radio Liberty Daily Report*, November 24, 1992, p. 2; and Pamela Pohling-Brown, "Iran's Subs Viewed with Unease," *International Defense Review*, February 1993, p. 150.

[21] See Cordesman, "Iran and Iraq: The Military Dimensions," p.32.

[22] For more on the Revolutionary Guard, see Kenneth Katzman, *The Warriors of Islam: Iran's Revolutionary Guard* (Boulder, Colo.: Westview Press, 1993).

[23] "Russia Set to Supply Iran, China With Nuclear Plants," *Wall Street Journal*, February 12, 1993, p. A10. Iran has signed an agreement with Russia for two 440 megawatts of electric power (MWe) VVERs (first generation, Russian pressurized water reactors) and with China for two

330 MWe pressurized water reactors (PWRs). Richard Masters, "On a Plateau After 50 Years," *Nuclear Engineering International*, June 1993, p. 21. For a lengthy discussion of VVERs, see hearing before the Senate Committee on Energy and Natural Resources, "Safety of Soviet-Designed Nuclear Powerplants," June 16, 1992, S. Hrg. 102-866.

[24] *Qol Yisra'el* (Israel), March 30, 1993, in FBIS-SOV, March 31, 1993, p. 71.

[25] For more on this point see Sokolski, "Iran: Willing to War," pp. 47-57.

[26] For details on Iraq's future military options see Michael Eisenstadt, *Like A Phoenix From the Ashes? The Future of Iraqi Military Power*, Policy Papers Number 36 (Washington, D.C.: The Washington Institute for Near East Policy, 1993).

[27] Cordesman, "Iran and Iraq: The Military Dimension," pp. 46-47.

[28] Ibid., p. 46.

[29] For details of the new U.S. Department of Defense Counterproliferation Initiative, see remarks by Les Aspin, Secretary of Defense, National Academy of Sciences, Committee on International Security and Arms Control, December 7, 1993.

[30] U.S. Department of State, *Patterns of Global Terrorism*, 1992, publication no. 10054, April 1993, pp. 1, 4.

[31] Rowland Evans and Robert Novak, "Iran's New Satellite," *Washington Post*, August 19, 1993, p. A29.

[32] Youssef Ibrahim, "Arabs Raise a Nervous Cry over Iranian Militancy," *New York Times*, December 21, 1992, p. A1, A10; see also Tom Post, "A New Alliance for Terror," *Newsweek*, February 24, 1992, p. 32. The United States listed Sudanese links to Abu Nidal, Hamas, An-Nahda of Tunisia, Libya and Iran. U.S. Department of State, *Patterns of Global Terrorism, 1991*, publication no. 9963, April 1992, p. 3. In December 1992, Egyptian Interior Minister Muhammad Abd-al-Halim Musa alleged that more than 2,000 Iranian guards were training Muslim extremists in

Sudan for planned terrorist attacks in Egypt. *Wall Street Journal*, December 3, 1992, p. A1.

[33] "Twenty-One Reported Killed In Nine Egyptian Raids on Muslim Militants," *New York Times*, March 11, 1993, p. A1; "Thousands in Egypt Mourn Police Killed by Militants," *Boston Globe*, April 13, 1993, p. 8.

[34] He emphasized this point during his April 1993 visit to the United States. He stated that Iran wants "to destabilize Egypt, just to keep Egypt away. We will never be kept away." (Transcript of *MacNeil/Lehrer NewsHour* interview with Mubarak, April 6, 1993, transcribed in Federal News Service, #L-06-02-E, p. 3.)

[35] Mubarak hinted in mid-November 1992 that Iran must cease all support of terrorism in Egypt. He told Parliament: "Iran should completely stop intervening in the internal affairs of Arab and Islamic countries. It is not the guardian of anyone and has no right to speak in the name of Islam and its teachings." "Egypt's Leader Decries Fundamentalists, Iran," *Boston Globe*, November 15, 1992, p. 2.

[36] The source revealed a plan to "strike at tourism and vital installations, assassinate..., create disturbances, and destabilize the country." *Middle East News Agency*, November 26, 1992, in FBIS-NES, November 27, 1992, p. 13.

[37] *Misr al-Fatah*, November 23, 1992, p. 1 in FBIS-NES, November 27, 1992, p. 13.

[38] Ibrahim, "Arabs Raise a Nervous Cry"; and *Al-Sharq Al-Awsat*, November 19, 1992, p. 1, in FBIS-NES, November 23, 1992, p. 52.

[39] "Algeria Breaks Diplomatic Ties with Iran," Reuters, March 27, 1993; an abbreviated version of the Reuters report appeared in "Algeria Breaks Ties with Iran," *New York Times*, March 28, 1993, p. 14.

[40] Elaine Sciolino, "Christopher Signals a Tougher U.S. Line toward Iran," *New York Times*, March 31, 1993, p. A3.

[41] Farhang is a professor of politics at Bennington College and is on the advisory board of the Middle East Watch. Farhang claimed that on June

10, 1993, an F.B.I. agent had informed him that Farhang is one of 200 names on an Iranian hit list. Mansour Farhang, "Iran Wants to Assassinate Me. Why?" *The New York Times*, December 8, 1993, p. A25.

[42] Anthony Parsons, "Iran and Western Europe," *Middle East Journal*, 43, no. 2 (Spring 1989) p. 223.

[43] U.S. Department of State, *Patterns of Global Terrorism, 1991*, p. 30. Other Iranian opposition figures who have been the victims of assassins include Massoud Kajavi, the brother of Mojahedin leader Kazem Rajavi in Geneva, Iranian Kurdish leader Abdul-Rahman Ghassemlou and his colleagues in Vienna, monarchist Cyrus Elahi, entertainer Fereidun Farrokhzad and Ghassemlou's successor, Sadegh Sharafkandi; "Conditions in Iran are Improving," letter to the editor, *The New York Times*, December 1, 1992, p. A24. Allegations of Iranian involvement have also surfaced in the deaths of Ayatollah Byhamadi, a former colonel in the Shah's intelligence service; Bahman Jauadi, a member of the Communist Party of Iran; and Bakhtiar supporters Ali Tabatabai and Abdol-Rahman Boroumand; Amnesty International, *Report 1990* (New York: Amnesty International, 1990), pp. 124-25; Henry Degenhardt, *Revolutionary and Dissident Movements* (London: Longman Group, 1988), p.167; and Arthur Banks, ed., *Political Handbook of the World, 1992* (Binghamton, N.Y.: CSA Publications, 1992), p. 359. In a 1993 attack, Mohammed Hussein Naghdi, an official with the National Council of Resistance, was gunned down in Rome on March 16, 1993. Although Iran has denied responsibility for the killing, senior U.S. officials said they had little doubt that Teheran ordered the assassination, adding that it reflected Iran's increased ability to carry out attacks abroad; Douglas Jehl, "Iran-Backed Terrorists Are Growing More Aggressive, U.S. Warns," *New York Times*, March 18, 1993, p. A8.

[44] "U.S. Sees Iranian Role in Buenos Aires Blast," *New York Times*, May 9, 1992, p. 3. The U.S. statement explained that "information has been gathered that indicates Iranian involvement in the attack, but there is not conclusive evidence at this time."

[45] "Car Bomb Kills Israeli Diplomat," *Washington Post*, March 8, 1992, p. A28.

[46] *Anatolia*, January 31, 1993, in FBIS-WEU, February 3, 1993, pp. 44-45.

[47] According to People's Mojahedin press releases, Ghorbani was kidnapped in June 1992, tortured and murdered with direction from Teheran. Also see "Turkey Asserts Islamic Ring That Killed Three Has Iran Links," *New York Times*, February 5, 1993, p. A6; and "Widow of Iranian Dissident Blames Teheran in His Death," *New York Times*, February 10, 1993, p. A14.

[48] U.S. Department of State, *Patterns of Global Terrorism, 1992*, pp. 38-39. *Voice of the Mojahed* reported on July 27, 1992, that Iran gives Hizbollah $35 million a year (FBIS-NES, July 30, 1992, p. 31).

[49] Jim Mann, "Senior U.S. Official Blames Iran for Fatal Hezbollah Bomb," *Los Angeles Times* (Washington edition), October 30, 1992, p. 3; and "Sabotage," *U.S. News & World Report*, November 23, 1992, p. 25.

[50] Patrick Clawson claims that Hamas will receive $15 million a year for two years from Iran. Patrick Clawson, "Hamas, Iran and the Radical Opposition to the Peace Process," *Policywatch*, peace watch no. 42, Washington Institute for Near East Policy, December 16, 1992. The *New York Times*, citing PLO leader Yasir Arafat, put Iran's contribution to Hamas at $20 million to $30 million thus far. Ibrahim, "Arabs Raise a Nervous Cry."

[51] U.S. Department of State, *Patterns of Global Terrorism, 1992*, pp. 37-38.

[52] U.S. Department of State, *Patterns of Global Terrorism, 1992*, p. 47.

[53] U.S. Department of State, *Patterns of Global Terrorism, 1992*, p. 46.

[54] IRNA, December 31, 1990, in FBIS-NES, January 2, 1991, p. 64; and IRIB Television Service, December 29, 1990, in FBIS-NES, January 2, 1991, pp. 64-65.

[55] *Voice of the Islamic Republic of Iran* (IRI), October 30, 1991; IRNA, October 30, 1991; and IRNA, October 30, 1991, in FBIS-NES, October 31, 1991, pp. 64-66.

[56] *Voice of the IRI*, September 18, 1992, in FBIS-NES, September 21, 1992, p. 55-56.

[57] *Al-Sharq Al-Awsat*, October 7, 1992, in FBIS-NES, October 8, 1992, p. 37; and *Sawt Al-Kuwayt Al-Duwali*, October 3, 1992, in FBIS-NES, October 6, 1992, p. 40.

[58] IRNA, July 26, 1993, in FBIS-NES, July, 27, 1993, p. 49; R. Jeffrey Smith, "Christopher to Pressure Syria to Block Cargo to Hezbollah," *Washington Post*, July 31, 1993, p. A14.

[59] Steven A. Holmes, "Christopher Says Middle East Talks Are Revived," *New York Times*, August 5, 1993, p. A6.

[60] Youssef Ibrahim, "Iranian Leader Denounces Peace Pact," *New York Times*, September 16, 1993, p. 10; and Andrew Borowiec, "Iran Seeks to Thwart PLO-Israeli Treaty," *Washington Times*, September 22, 1993, p. A14.

IRANIAN HUMAN RIGHTS ABUSES

[1] The Baha'i faith was founded in the mid-nineteenth century. The Baha'i religion teaches that all religions lead to an identical truth; Baha'i therefore believe in the unity of all religions. The founder of Baha'i, Baha Ullah, was the latest in a series of divine manifestations that include Jesus, Muhammad, Zoroaster and the Buddha. The spelling of Baha'i has been standardized throughout this report. For more information on the Baha'i, see *Encyclopedia Britannica*, 15th ed., s.v. "Baha'i faith." The Iranian government considers the Baha'i to be heretics. See "A Death in Iran," *New York Times*, August 18, 1992, p. A18.

[2] Released in December 1993, the 1994 Freedom House ratings place Iran and its neighbors at the bottom of the world in terms of political rights and civil liberties. In combined average ratings ranging from one (most free) to seven (least free), Iran scored a 6.5; this was matched by Qatar and Algeria. Scoring lower with a 7 were Afghanistan, Iraq, Libya, Saudi Arabia, Sudan and Syria. Other regional scores: Israel (2), Israeli-occupied territories (5.5), Jordan (4), Pakistan (4), Turkey (4), Yemen (4.5), Kuwait (5), Morocco (5), Lebanon (5.5), Bahrain (6), Egypt (6), Oman (6) and UAE (6). Except for Lebanon, countries and territories

rated 5.5 to 7 are included in Freedom House's not free category. Appendix III of this Iran report reviews the 1993 Freedom House scores. For the 1994 scores, see "Combined Average Ratings — Independent Countries" and "Combined Average Ratings — Related Territories," *Freedom Review*, 25, no. 1, January-February, 1994, pp. 20-21.

[3] "Iran Returns to the World," *The Economist*, April 18, 1992, p. 15.

UNITED STATES POLICY: RECOMMENDATIONS

[1] See Lake, "Confronting Backlash States."

IRAN'S GEOGRAPHY AND THE LOGISTICS OF CENTRAL ASIA

[1] Most statistical information is taken from *Encyclopedia Britannica*, 15th ed., s.v. "Iran."

[2] Amuzegar, "The Iranian Economy," p. 419.

[3] James Tanner and Bhushan Bahree, "OPEC Members Agree on Quotas For Oil Output," *Wall Street Journal*, September 30, 1993, p. A5.

[4] Robin Wright, *In the Name of God* (New York: Simon and Schuster, 1989), p. 24.

[5] *Encyclopedia Britannica*, 15th ed., s.v. "Iran"; "New World Order: Water to the Land," *Asiaweek*, March 24, 1993, p. 20.

[6] Amuzegar, "The Iranian Economy," p. 418.

[7] *The Europa World Year Book 1992*, vol. 1 (London: Europa Publications Limited, 1992), p. 1,434.

[8] *The World Factbook 1992* (Washington, D.C.: Central Intelligence Agency, 1992), p. 161.

[9] Map Link classified roads as "most important road," "connecting road" and "secondary road." This terminology, listed in descending order of quality, is repeated here. Map Link is based in Santa Barbara, California.

[10] *The Europa World Year Book 1992*, vol. 1, p. 1,434.

[11] The report neither identified the exact path of the new route nor indicated whether it is open or under construction. IRNA, September 10, 1992, in FBIS-SOV, September 11, 1992, p. 40.

[12] *Voice of the Islamic Republic of Iran*, May 9, 1992 in FBIS-NES, May 12, 1992, p. 45.

[13] Felix Corley, "Armenia and Iran," *Middle East International*, August 28, 1993, p. 15.

[14] Both figures were given by Sadiq Afshar, managing director of Iran's state railways company, at the twenty-sixth Middle East Railways Conference in Teheran. IRNA, November 1, 1992 in FBIS-NES, November 4, 1992, p. 56. *The Europa World Yearbook 1992* noted 4,847 kilometers of track (vol. 1, p. 1,434).

[15] According to a May 1993 communication with David Briginshaw, associate editor of the *International Railway Journal and Rapid Transit Review*, Pakistani Railways offered in 1992 to extend the Kerman-Zahedan line. He was unsure if the offer led to any agreement, but an undated map of the Iranian rail system provided by Briginshaw did not show any construction. The 1992 *National Geographic Atlas*, completed in December 1991, shows the line under construction. The 1992-93 *Jane's World Railways* claims that "In the spring of 1991 agreement was reached with Pakistan Railways to undertake joint construction of a 375 km line from Kerman to Zahedan" but notes no further progress. The atlas is apparently in error.

[16] Although the *National Geographic Atlas* shows that the Sirjan-Bandar Abbas line (the southern portion of the Bafq-Bandar Abbas rail line) has been completed, Briginshaw and *Jane's World Railways* assert that it is under construction using Pakistani rail contractors and should open in 1994. In early 1994, Parviz Alivand, deputy director of the Iranian railways organization, predicted that the Bafq-Bander Abbas link would be ready by the spring of 1995. "General Electric," *MEED*, vol. 38, no. 5, February 4, 1994, p. 15.

[17] *Voice of the Islamic Republic of Iran*, May 15, 1992, in FBIS-NES, May 15, 1992.

[18] IRNA, May 16, 1992 in FBIS-NES, May 20, 1992, p. 52. For more recent Iranian-Georgian discussions on transportation on major bodies of water, see IRNA, January 21, 1993 in FBIS-NES, January 22, 1993, p. 59.

[19] IRNA, July 21, 1992, in FBIS-NES, July 23, 1992, pp. 57-58.

[20] *The Middle East Today*, No. 298 (transmitted by facsimile), July 8, 1992.

[21] *Voice of the Islamic Republic of Iran*, June 6, 1992, in FBIS-NES, June 8, 1992, p. 13. The text referred to the Marv-Tajan railway.

[22] IRNA, February 3, 1993, in FBIS-SOV, February 3, 1993, p. 47.

[23] *Voice of the Islamic Republic of Iran*, June 23, 1993, in FBIS-NES, June 24, 1993, p. 36. On Turkmenistan rail construction, see "Tehran Expands Links with Republics," *MEED*, vol. 36, no. 4, January 31, 1992, p. 19.

[24] IRNA, November 1, 1992 in FBIS-NES, November 4, 1992, p. 56; and "High Speed Tehran-Isfahan Rail Line Proposed," *MEED*, vol. 37, no. 12, March 26, 1993, p. 22.

[25] IRNA, June 21, 1992 in FBIS-NES, June 26, 1992, p. 51.

[26] Steve Coll, "Central Asia's High-Stakes Oil Game," *Washington Post*, May 9, 1993, pp. A1, A28; "Turkey Claims the Oil Route," *The Middle East*, May 1993, p. 9; and James Dorsey, "Armenia to Sign Accord with Iran for Natural Gas," *Washington Times*, April 2, 1993, p. A10.

THE RUSHDIE AFFAIR

[1] Reprinted in Daniel Pipes, "The Ayatollah, the Novelist, and the West," *Commentary*, June 1989, p. 12.

[2] Daniel Pipes outlines the initial responses of the Western governments in *The Rushdie Affair* (New York: Carol Publishing Group, 1990), pp. 155-59.

[3] Pipes, "The Ayatollah, the Novelist, and the West," p. 14.

[4] Ibid.

[5] Steven Prokesch, "Iran Sees Time Nearing for New Ties to Britain," *New York Times*, August 4, 1990, p. A7.

[6] Paul Lewis, "Britain and Iran Announce Renewal of Ties Broken over Rushdie Affair," *New York Times*, September 28, 1990, p. A7.

[7] Chris Hedges, "Rushdie Seeks to Mend His Rift with Islam," *New York Times*, December 25, 1990, p. 9.

[8] William E. Schmidt, "Britain and Iran Harden Positions on Rushdie," *New York Times*, February 15, 1993, p. A3.

[9] "Iran's Indecent Proposal," *New York Times*, February 16, 1993, p. A16 and "Blessed to Kill," *Boston Globe*, February 17, 1993, p. 14.

[10] William Miller, "Major Sets Meeting With Rushdie in Bid to Press Iran on Threat," *Boston Globe*, April 13, 1993, p. 8.

[11] Eugene Robinson, "Rushdie Meets with John Major," *Washington Post*, May 12, 1993, p. B2; William Miller, "Rushdie Hails Talks with Major," *Boston Globe*, May 12, 1993, p. 2.

[12] "Iran's Indecent Proposal," *New York Times*, February 16, 1993, p. A16.

[13] Eugene Robinson, "Norwegian Publisher of 'Satanic Verses' Is Shot," *Washington Post*, October 12, 1993, p. A13.

[14] Douglas Jehl, "No Disrespect Meant to Islam President Says," *New York Times*, December 1, 1993, pp. A1, A6.

REPORTS OF GOVERNMENTAL AND PRIVATE ORGANIZATIONS ON HUMAN RIGHTS IN IRAN

[1] Some human rights reports rely on the research and investigative work of others.

[2] U.N. General Assembly, Forty-eighth session, *Situation of Human Rights in the Islamic Republic of Iran: Note by the Secretary-General*, prepared by R. G. Pohl pursuant to paragraph 13 of Commission on Human Rights resolution 1993/62; document no. A/48/526, November 8, 1993.

[3] Paul Lewis, "U.N. Rebukes Myanmar Leaders on Human Rights and Democracy," *New York Times*, December 7, 1993, p. A10.

[4] U.N. Commission on Human Rights, Forty-ninth session, *Situation of Human Rights in the Islamic Republic of Iran*, prepared by Reynaldo Galindo Pohl pursuant to paragraph 13 of Commission on Human Rights resolution 1992/67; document no. E/CN.4/1993/41, January 28, 1993. A similar interim report was issued on November 13, 1992.

[5] U.N. Commission on Human Rights, Forty-ninth session, *Situation of Human Rights in the Islamic Republic of Iran*, resolution adopted by the Commission on Human Rights on March 10, 1993; document no. E/CN.4/1993/L.35, March 4, 1993. The resolution was adopted with 23 votes for, 11 against and 14 abstaining.

[6] U.N. General Assembly, Forty-seventh session, *Situation of Human Rights in the Islamic Republic of Iran: Note by the Secretary-General*, prepared by R. G. Pohl; document no. A/47/617, November 13, 1992.

[7] U.S. Department of State, *Country Reports on Human Rights Practices for 1992* (Washington, D.C.: U.S. Government Printing Office, 1993), pp. 999-1,006.

[8] *Human Rights Watch World Report 1993* (New York: Human Rights Watch, December, 1992), pp. 300-5. The report covers January through November 1992.

[9] For the Amnesty evaluation of Iran in 1991, see Amnesty International, *Report 1992: A Comprehensive Report on Human Rights Violations around the World* (New York: Amnesty International, 1992), pp. 144-46.

[10] Amnesty International, "Iran: Executions of Prisoners Continue Unabated," Amnesty International Index: MDE 13/18/92, October 1, 1992.

[11] Amnesty International, "Iran: Unfair Trials of Political Detainees," MDE 13/15/92, July 1992.

[12] Amnesty International, "Iran: Imprisonment, Torture and Execution of Political Opponents," MDE 13/01/92, January 1992.

[13] R. Bruce McColm (survey coordinator), *Freedom in the World, Political Rights and Civil Liberties, 1991-1992* (New York: Freedom House, 1992), pp. 251-56, 572-73. Also see earlier endnote for 1994 data.

[14] Population Action International, "The International Human Suffering Index" (pamphlet) (Washington, D.C.: Population Action International, 1992).

U.S. OPERATIONAL POLICY TOWARD IRAN

[1] U.S. Department of State, "Country Reports on Economic Policy and Trade Practices," report submitted to the House Committee on Foreign Affairs, the House Committee on Ways and Means, the Senate Committee on Foreign Relations, and the Senate Committee on Finance (Washington, D.C.: U.S. Government Printing Office, February 1993) p. 724.

[2] U.S. Department of Commerce, *1993 Annual Foreign Policy Report to Congress* (Washington, D.C.: U.S. Government Printing Office, February 1, 1993) pp. 17-26. The Commerce report gives detailed analysis of export controls and antiterrorism restraints.

[3] For executive order, see "Blocking Iranian Government Property" executive order number 12170, November 14, 1979, in *Public Papers of the Presidents of the United States: Jimmy Carter, 1979*, vol. 2 (Washington, D.C.: U.S. Government Printing Office, 1980), p. 2,118. For the latest renewal see "Notice on Continuation of Iran Emergency," October 25, 1992, in *Weekly Compilation of Presidential Documents*, November 2, 1992, p. 2,123.

[4] "Sanctions Against Iran," April 7, 1980, in *Public Papers of the Presidents of the United States: Jimmy Carter, 1980-81*, vol. 1 (Washington, D.C.: U.S. Government Printing Office, 1981), p. 611; and U.S. Department of State, *Diplomatic List* (Washington, D.C.: U.S. Government Printing Office, January 1993), p. 49.

[5] The U.S. presidential statements and orders of January 19, 1981, setting up the process can be found in *Public Papers of the Presidents of the United States: Jimmy Carter, 1980-81*, vol. 3 (Washington, D.C.: U.S. Government Printing Office, 1982), pp. 3,026-43. Other sources include Kate Gillespie, "U.S. Companies and Iran at the Hague," *Middle East Journal*,

vol. 44, no. 1, Winter, 1990, p. 22; "Update on U.S.-Iran Claims Settlement," *Department of State Bulletin*, November 1989, p. 60; Elaine Sciolino, "U.S. and Iran Sign a Compensation Pact," *New York Times*, November 28, 1991, p. A3; Elaine Sciolino, "U.S. Near Deal With Iranians on Arms Funds," *New York Times*, November 21, 1991, p. A15; "Letter to Congressional Leaders on the National Emergency with Respect to Iran," November 29, 1990, in *Public Papers of the Presidents of the United States: George Bush, 1990*, vol. 2 (Washington, D.C.: U.S. Government Printing Office, 1991), pp. 1,705-7; "Message to the Congress Reporting on the National Emergency with Respect to Iran," May 14, 1992, in *Weekly Compilation of Presidential Documents*, May 18, 1992, pp. 861-63; "Letter to Congressional Leaders Reporting on the National Emergency with Respect to Iran," November 10, 1992, in *Weekly Compilation of Presidential Documents*, November 16, 1992, pp. 2,294-95; and "Message to the Congress Reporting on the National Emergency with Respect to Iran," November 10, 1993, in *Weekly Compilation of Presidential Documents*, November 15, 1993, pp. 2,321-23.

[6] "January 23," *Department of State Bulletin*, March, 1984, p. 77. The designation was published on January 23 in *The Federal Register*.

[7] Foreign Assistance Act, U.S. Code, vol. 22, sec. 2371 (annual).

[8] Arms Export Control Act, U.S. Code, vol. 22, secs. 2778 and 2780 (1971 and subsequent amendments).

[9] Export Administration Act, U.S. Code, vol. 50, app. 2401 (1979). President Bush issued executive order number 12730 on September 30, 1990, declaring a national emergency "to deal with the threat to the national security and foreign policy of the United States caused by the lapse of the Export Administration Act of 1979." This was superseded by the act's extension in Public Law 103-10 (March 27, 1993). See the revocation of executive order 12730 in "Executive Order 12867—Termination of Emergency Authority for Certain Export Controls," September 30, 1993, in *Weekly Compilation of Presidential Documents*, October 4, 1993, p. 1,935.

[10] Enacted as section 555 of the Foreign Operations, Export Financing, and Related Programs Appropriations Act, 1991 (Public Law 101-513; 104 Stat. 2021; enacted November 5, 1990).

11 "White House Fact Sheet," *Department of State Bulletin*, December 1987, pp. 75-76.

12 For the initial order, see "Executive Order 12613—Prohibiting Imports from Iran," October 29, 1987, in *Public Papers of the Presidents of the United States: Ronald Reagan, 1987*, vol. 2 (Washington, D.C.: U.S. Government Printing Office, 1989), pp. 1,244-45 (related messages appear on pp. 1,232, 1,245-46). Also see "Message to the Congress Reporting on the National Emergency with Respect to Iran," June 7, 1988, in *Public Papers of the Presidents of the United States: Ronald Reagan, 1988*, vol. 1 (Washington, D.C.: U.S. Government Printing Office, 1990), pp. 737-40; and Christine Lawrence, ed., *1987 CQ Almanac* (Washington, D.C.: Congressional Quarterly, 1988), p. 664.

13 Public Law 102-484, October 23, 1992.

14 Carroll J. Doherty, "Aid Bill Moves Smoothly Into Law Despite Crisis in Russia," *CQ*, October 2, 1993, p. 2,661.

15 The Foreign Operations, Export Financing and Related Programs Appropriations Act, 1993 was enacted on October 6, 1992 and became Public Law 102-391; the Baha'i resolution, H. Con. Res. 156, passed in the House on June 2, 1992, and in the Senate on July 2, 1992; Rep. Schumer sponsored H.R. 1708; Rep. Gejdenson sponsored H.R. 2318; and Rep. Kyl sponsored H.R. 5779.

16 "Travel to Iran," *Department of State Bulletin*, March 1981, p. 17; and "Iran—Consular Information Sheet," U.S. Department of State, August 31, 1993, 93-214.

17 See especially 50 U.S. Code 191 (1982). Also see Barry E. Carter, *International Economic Sanctions* (Cambridge, England: Cambridge University Press, 1988), pp. 56-57. Carter's book is an excellent primer on the potential range of U.S. controls and restrictions. Also see "Statement by Press Secretary Fitzwater on Foreign Access to United States Ports," May 8, 1991, in *Public Papers of the Presidents of the United States: George Bush, 1991*, vol. 1 (Washington, D.C.: U.S. Government Printing Office, 1992), p. 484.

18 "We Win! Commerce Department Stops Review of Iranian CVD," *Western Pistachio News*, Summer 1992, p. 11; and Albert Mark, "The Pistachio War: U.S. Growers Fight Imports From Iran," *Wall Street Journal*, November 6, 1985, pp. 1, 22.

INDEX